# DIVINE INTERVENTION

## *An Unexpected Journey from Chaos to Clarity*

### SUSAN ANDERSON

**BEYOND
WORDS**
*Publishing*
I N C

Beyond Words Publishing, Inc.
20827 N.W. Cornell Road, Suite 500
Hillsboro, Oregon 97124-9808
503-531-8700
1-800-284-9673

Proofreaders: Joseph Siegel and Lori Stephens
Editor: Ann Hauser
Cover design: Susan Shankin
Interior design and composition: Heather Speight
Managing editor: Kathy Matthews


Printed in the United States of America
Distributed to the book trade by Publishers Group West


Library of Congress Cataloging-in-Publication Data
Anderson, Susan, 1944–
    Divine intervention : an unexpected journey from chaos to clarity
/ Susan Anderson.
      p. cm.
    ISBN 1-58270-000-1 (trade paper)
    1. Psychiatric hospital care—Personal narratives. 2. Mysticism—
Psychology 3. Experience (Religion) 4. Spiritual life.
    I. Title
RC439.2.A53 1999
616.89—dc21                                                    98-37211
                                                                   CIP

The corporate mission of Beyond Words Publishing, Inc.:
Inspire to Integrity

# DIVINE
# INTERVENTION

# CONTENTS

FOREWORD       ix

INTRODUCTION       xiii

| | | |
|---|---|---|
| 1. | Inferno | 1 |
| 2. | To Alice Miller | 13 |
| 3. | Jane's Pain | 21 |
| 4. | Mutiny | 29 |
| 5. | Bob and Sue | 41 |
| 6. | Betrayed | 53 |
| 7. | Special Relationships | 65 |
| 8. | Divine Lightning | 77 |
| 9. | Mind Wars | 87 |
| 10. | Sawtooth Nightmare Plunge | 97 |
| 11. | Volcanoes and Other Lessons | 109 |
| 12. | Challenges | 121 |
| 13. | The Rose Window | 131 |
| 14. | Miracles in a Silver Cloud | 141 |
| 15. | Saint Bernadette | 153 |
| 16. | Over the Edge | 163 |
| 17. | Paradiso | 173 |
| 18. | Illumination | 183 |

EPILOGUE       193

AFTERWORD       197

*Our greatest blessings come to us by way of madness,*
*provided the madness is given us by divine gift.*

—SOCRATES

# FOREWORD

As a psychologist, I find Susan Anderson's story to be a compelling example of what we call "spiritual emergency" (Grof and Grof). A spiritual emergency occurs when a person is so overwhelmed by encounters with religious or spiritual phenomena that his/her psychological, social, and occupational functioning are disrupted. What happened to Susan is the stuff of spiritual myth and religious history. Oddly, these mysterious spiritual anomalies seem to be increasing in contemporary society.

Most spirits emerge gradually. A few seem to burst forth in a kind of aggressive release of the soul. We see this in the proverbial blinding flash of sudden, overwhelming Christian conversions. Another good example, from the spirituality of India, is Kundalini awakening, where one can be overcome by a rush of electrical energy that travels from the base of the spine to the brain, erupting in a classic duel between dark and light. There are many paths and processes of spiritual emergence, but the resulting transformation to a new life of underlying peace and joy is universal.

As spirituality is one of the world's most basic cultural components, many colleagues and I have long seen a need for the mental health system to validate the spiritual aspects of human behavior. In the early twentieth century, C. G. Jung laid the groundwork for this important inclusion, but most clinicians, influenced by atheist Freud and the growing "prove it" school of science, either ignored or pathologized it.

However, a major breakthrough came in 1991 when a *DSM-IV* Task Force was formed to revise psychiatry's "Bible," the *Diagnostic and Statistical Manual of Mental Disorders III* (*DSM-III*). Two psychiatrists, Robert Turner and Francis G. Lu, and I proposed to the Task Force that the *DSM-IV* for the first time include a category for religious and spiritual problems. After a great deal of debate, it was added.

Our proposal was based on our increasing encounters with patients who were having religious or spiritual crises. At their most severe, these could resemble psychotic episodes. These patients inevitably returned to normal states with improved lives—not possible with most mental illness, which is nearly always chronic. It is important that therapists learn to recognize the differences between psychosis and mystical experience so that a patient who is having a life-altering spiritual episode is not misdiagnosed, perhaps even hospitalized, as mentally ill.

As I read *Divine Intervention* I realized that this was exactly what happened to Susan. She involuntarily journeyed through a series of strange and powerful spiritual events—a complete departure from her normal life. So confused and panicked did she become that she turned to the medical community for help. They were unable to assist her in her spiritual crisis. She became convinced that she was developing mental illness and ended up on a psychiatric ward.

Blessed with loving family and friends and a very sharp, open mind, Susan was able to integrate this experience into her life in a positive way. Then, like Joseph Campbell's mythological heroes and the shamans of ancient cultures, she returned to society awestruck, moved by a deep new wisdom that she longed to share to better the world. Fortunately for us, she does so very convincingly in this moving book.

As Susan realizes, the best thing we can do to achieve a happy life is to continue to reach for that elusive state of grace that we instinctively know exists beyond our rational thoughts. This book shows us effective ways to find and open up to powerful sources of help and inspiration—so we can all benefit from *Divine Intervention*.

DAVID LUKOFF, PH.D.

PETALUMA, CALIFORNIA, JULY 1998

# INTRODUCTION

C hristmas 1984 was a celebration of sugar and shop- ping for my children and me. I had never learned religious rituals, had never heard my parents say the word "God." Had someone told me that overpowering spiritual energy was about to possess me, that I would someday be teaching Sunday school, taking a ministry class and placing an altar in my living room, I would have told them that they were crazy!

Just after that Christmas, I entered a three-day period of spiritual trauma. For the next four years, I searched for answers. Then, in the spring of 1989, I endured forty days of spiritual events so disturbing that I found myself locked up on a mental ward in a temporary psychotic state. In this darkest place on Earth, divine intervention helped me com- plete my transformation.

I was astounded to learn that thousands of people are having religious and spiritual experiences similar to mine and are emerging with a glorious new way of living and being. Also like me, many people feel confused and disturbed enough to seek professional help, and many are misunderstood or misdiagnosed. The good news is that therapists and society in general are at last becoming edu- cated about this resurgent phenomenon.

I have written my story to contribute to this education. I also hope it demonstrates how desperately we need to embrace a cohesive new spirit in modern culture, a spirit that embraces and honors our differences and our oneness. Most of all, I pray that it inspires readers to believe that God exists—as our courage, our ability, and our calling to grow from our personal traumas, to create a better world, and to love one another.

# ONE

# INFERNO

*... transformational crises are often suppressed by routine psychiatric care, medication, and even institutionalization.*

—Dr. Stanislav Grof, Psychiatrist

Thursday, April 13, 1989—Midmorning: When I heard the unmistakable click of a dead bolt behind me, I realized for the first time what was really happening to me. There's only one part of a hospital where people are locked up—the psych ward. I turned around and looked frantically from my personal physician, Dr. Barbara Ryan, who had brought me here, to the green-clad attendant. He had opened the double doors as we approached, obviously expecting us. Feeling like a trapped animal, my terror and fury were instantaneous, but I was numb, paralyzed, unable to speak.

Dr. Ryan mistook my dumbness for acceptance. "So, here we are," she said. Her tone was patronizing. She smiled nervously. "I'm sure you will be treated well and be just fine here," she continued, glancing toward the locked doors. They were heavy doors with wire reinforced windows in them.

I barely heard her. My already overloaded mind was reeling. I tried to focus my eyes on the attendant who was filling out the form Dr. Ryan had given him. He looked to be about thirty-something and was large and powerful. He completed the form and handed it to Dr. Ryan, then turned to stare at me, his face taut and unsmiling. His plastic name-tag said "Steve."

Firmly grasping my arm, Steve said, "If you'll just come with me, Ms. Brewster, we'll get you settled." His voice was low but threatening. Still shocked and speechless, I gave a long, last desperate glance at Dr. Ryan, who was looking at the floor, then allowed him to squire me down the long, green corridor.

As we approached a nurses' station, Steve stopped me and called out to another attendant, a young woman dressed in that same green uniform. She wordlessly came and took my purse and books from me (just before leaving for the hospital, I had grabbed my Bible and another glori-ous holy book called *A Course in Miracles*). She then disap-peared with them through a door in the back of the nurses' station. I felt ravaged by her taking them but helpless to stop it.

We proceeded to the end of the hall where we turned left into a stark room, which was also painted dull green. It contained a couple of metal hospital beds. "Sit here," Steve told me, indicating the bed nearer the door. Then, still with-out a smile or one word of welcome or explanation, he left the room, closing the massive, heavy door behind him. This door had neither lock nor latch, but I clearly got that I was not to leave.

Still too scared to protest, I sat heavily on the bed, assuming someone would come and tell me exactly what to expect at any moment. I felt exhausted and confused. There must be some mistake, I thought. I don't understand why I'm here. I had envisioned being on a regular hospital ward, talking periodically with kindly doctor/counselors who would guide and cure me. It had never occurred to me that I would be locked up.

I looked around the room. A lampless metal night-stand and a metal side chair with a green vinyl seat were beside each bed. There were also two steel locker-type clos-

2

ets against the opposite wall. I got up and walked over to the single window. I saw that it looked out on the Eastside Freeway. I watched the cars whizzing by for a few moments. Suddenly I noticed that a row of vertical metal bars was embedded in the casing outside the glass. I realized with a profound shock that I had never had my freedom to come and go at will taken away before. I felt massive waves of some feeling I couldn't identify wash over and over me. I felt nauseated, like I might faint.

I returned to sit on the bed, wishing I had a watch. It seemed as though twenty or thirty minutes passed. I began to feel a whole new terror. The realization that I was on a mental ward—where they put crazy people—began to sink in. Again I felt there must obviously have been some miscommunication. I had a million questions to ask, if anyone ever came to answer them!

As I waited on and on, I began to feel increasingly infuriated with the way I was being ignored. I couldn't believe that I couldn't just get up and leave. Then, at some point, I began to question myself. My rage and frustration alternated with immense fear, to which I added a new emotion: guilt. This must be what it's like to be admitted to prison, I thought. I feel like I've done something wrong, for God's sake. Who in the hell are these people, and what right do they have to treat me this way?!

I tried to calm my rampaging emotions so my mind could figure out how this had happened. I had cried out for help to a trusted doctor whom I had known for four years. How could she have done this to me without my knowledge? Nothing made sense at this point. I sat waiting, feeling increasingly resigned and depressed. I was alone with no solace, no welcome, and no idea of what to expect for what seemed like hours. Actually, it was probably about an hour before a woman entered the room without knocking.

She pulled up a metal chair and sat facing me as I sat on the bed. "I'm Dr. Tanner," she said. "I will be your psychiatrist here." She was detached, cool. Like Dr. Ryan, she was close to my age. She had short, light hair, fair freckled skin, and faded blue eyes that were magnified by thick glasses. "And you are Susan Brewster?"

I could not muster much desire to respond. I did not even know for sure who I was. It seemed like they had taken away my identity and my humanness somehow. I heard my voice coming out in a dull, exhausted whisper. It was hard to breathe, and each word seemed to require great effort. I looked at the floor. "Why am I in this place?"

Suddenly, I felt a little surge of indignation. I lifted my head and looked Dr. Tanner in the eye, but she spoke before I could repeat my question. "Why don't you tell me what happened and how you are feeling," she said. She was maddeningly calm.

I felt no warmth or concern coming from this woman. Doesn't anybody ever smile around here? I thought. I did not feel like cooperating with her. I wanted her to answer my questions. She looked steadily back at me. My courage waned again, and my deeply ingrained patterning to obey authority kicked in. I remembered my extreme emotional highs and lows of the last few weeks. "I think I'm manic-depressive," I finally whispered.

"What makes you think that?" she asked. She raised one eyebrow slightly, and I thought she still sounded clinical and unfeeling.

"I don't want to talk about it," I said, feeling yet another resurgence of righteous wrath. I sat up straighter and leaned toward her. "I don't need to be locked up. I asked to come here for help, not to be locked up. I want to leave here immediately!" I realized that I was yelling.

She just stared at me for a few moments. "I am going to prescribe something to help you get some rest," she said. "We'll talk again later."

She rose and left the room. I threw myself down on the bed, my frustration and anxiety increasing by the moment.

I curled into fetal position facing the wall. After a few minutes, I heard someone come into the room and approach my bed. I rolled over to see a nurse, bustly and stern in a traditional white uniform, standing over me with a hypodermic needle poised in one raised hand.

"If you'll just pull down your drawers, Ms. Brewster," she said, "Doctor wants you to have something to help you rest." I certainly did not feel I had a choice. She was as grim and determined and intimidating as everyone else was here. Besides, rest sounded good. I bared my rump and she deftly gave me the shot, then left without another word.

I lay back, waiting for the drug to soothe and relax me, but instead, my agitation began to increase. I had feared myself insane more than once in the past few weeks, but I had never completely lost touch with reality. Sometimes objects had appeared to become ultra bright and shimmery, but nothing ever went away or became something else. The drug that was supposed to help me made me completely lose touch, sending me to some dark nightmare world.

I felt like I began writhing around on the hospital bed, like I couldn't stop, couldn't stay present. My thoughts became bizarre and violent. I hallucinated unnamed black figures coming at me. Many of my thoughts were sexual; I felt like I was inserting objects into my vagina and screaming and screaming.

Then it seemed like I was gasping and panting, calling out over and over, very rapidly, "Oh, my God! Oh, my God! Oh, my God! I'm in a mental hospital! I will never have friends! I will never have a family! I will never get married! I will never have a job! I'm going to die! I'm insane! I'm going to die! No one even knows I'm here! I need to die! It's the only way out of here!"

I do not know how long I remained in this frantic state. Gradually, I began to return to the reality of the hospital room. I lay on my bed, limp and exhausted. I cried off and on but fought the tears, determined not to let them see me

5

defeated. Steve opened my door and looked in. "Do you want to talk?" he asked. He sounded professional and uncaring to me, and I was still furious with him and everyone else there. Besides, I was horrified to think that he might have seen or heard any of what I had recently experienced as a result of the medication. I still had no idea if I had actually been screaming out loud or if it had all been in my mind. I did not respond and he left.

I continued to feel alternately depressed and panicky. All the horror stories were true, I thought; they lock you up and give you hideous drugs to shut you up when you protest. I lay on my bed for the next couple of hours of that first fateful day, completely spent and darkly anxious.

Months after this time, I heard a psychiatrist lecturing on the process of inducting individuals into prison, the armed forces, and mental hospitals. He said that these people are stripped of all personal identity and reduced to the status of objects or numbers in a calculated dehumanization process. He also said that locking someone up in a bare room when they come to a hospital for healing would make the sanest person experience a level of humiliation, frustration, and rage that would easily justify the one protest left to them in that situation: smearing their own feces on the walls. This, of course, is seen as further proof of their insanity. I could understand how someone would do this.

This day of my admission to the hospital was a Thursday in the spring of 1989. I had called Dr. Ryan at 2 A.M. that same morning thinking that I had reached the absolute end of my endurance. I was no longer able to cope with the exhaustion and terror. No one had been able to explain the bizarre events that had been happening to me. I had realized that I needed to go somewhere to rest and regain my physical and mental strength so I could figure out what was wrong with me.

I had expected to be treated with kindness wherever I went, however. I felt instead that I had been neglected and abused. I certainly had not felt cared for when they locked me up without informing me, abandoned me for an hour to worry about my fate, then administered a drug that gave me hideous nightmares without warning me. Not one person had said a kind word to me. Even Steve's offer to talk had seemed more like a challenge to me than an offer of support. I felt like he was really saying, "Are you ready to admit that you are screwed up?"

Suddenly, just when I thought getting any help in this place was completely hopeless, something happened that began to shift things for me. I heard the door swish open. Someone tiptoed in and approached the bed. Now what do they want? I thought. I was still facing the wall and pretended to be asleep. I heard a soft thud close to my head, then they left. After a while, I raised up and turned my head to see what had made the sound. My Bible, my *Course in Miracles*, and my purse were on the nightstand. I lay back down.

At that moment, somehow, because I knew those books were there, my rage and terror began very, very slowly to abate. A tiny ray of light infiltrated the total blackness of my consciousness, then grew brighter and stronger. Finally, I rolled over and reached for the books, just clutching them to me for a long while, tears running down my face. My thoughts became more ordered and some strength began to seep back into my depleted mind and body.

I was still too unfocused to read, but I began to remember the immense comfort I had gotten from these books the past few days. I remembered asking the God they talked about to help me, because for the first time in my life, I couldn't seem to figure out how to help myself. I asked God for help now.

Though I soon felt stronger and more peaceful, I continued to believe that I was in the wrong place and that I needed to get out as soon as possible. I didn't see how I could get the help I needed in a place where I was abused

7

with drugs and treated with such cold, uncaring suspicion and total lack of respect.

There was a wall phone located in the corridor. I began calling everyone I knew to appeal for rescue. All my friends and my children were indignant and sympathetic, promising to do what they could as soon as possible, but then a strange thing would happen—subsequent calls reflected corroboration with the enemy. They all told me they talked to Dr. Ryan or the hospital staff who told them I was where I needed to be and not to worry; it is normal for people to protest and try to get out.

My frustration and anxiety were again approaching some sort of tolerance limit, when, sometime in the late afternoon, I reached my mother in California. There was something about that voice saying the perfect things: "There's some sort of mistake, Honey. Don't worry about a thing. I'm on my way to get you out of there. Get some sleep and I'll take care of everything when I get there."

Thank my newfound God, my mother would get me out of here. I felt as though I had been removed from a vise grip and dropped into warm water—right back into the womb. I let go. I gave up. I relaxed back onto my bed and slept for an hour or so.

I awoke to the sounds of voices and clattering dishes outside my room. An attendant came to my door to tell me I could come out and get a dinner tray and go eat in the eating room with the other patients. I was hungry in spite of my continuing duress. The food was typical hospital fare—bland meat loaf, packaged mashed potatoes, and overcooked green beans. It tasted great to me.

Finishing, I looked around the little room at the other patients. I felt somehow different from my fellow lockup crazies from that very first dinner hour. I couldn't figure out exactly what it was. They seemed somehow disinterested in me, absorbed totally in their own inner worlds. I, on the

8

other hand, found them all fascinating, wondering why each of them was in this place.

After dinner, I returned to my room feeling more relaxed than I had all day. My mind free of terror for the moment, I stood staring out the window at the cars speeding along the freeway. A cantaloupe-colored sun was setting on the horizon above them. I was absorbed in the scene and didn't hear Dr. Tanner open my door. She spoke in that maddeningly calm voice, "Do you feel like talking for a moment, Susan?"

I felt collected enough to talk to her this evening. I returned to the bed while she sat in the chair. I told her some of what had been occurring for me for the last few weeks. I showed her my books and told her repeatedly how many of my most powerful experiences had been spiritual. She responded to this with expressions of doubt, "Hmm, well I don't know if that is really significant." I felt misunderstood, invalidated. When I described how my legs had sometimes been so paralyzed that I couldn't walk, she said, "Well, that must have been difficult for you." Her tone sounded patronizing to me.

I then told her about my reading Dr. Carl Rogers and other humanistic psychologists and my belief in loving therapy. She frowned, saying, "I've heard of such things, but we didn't learn much about them in medical school. We were taught to remain very detached from patients. I'm afraid my training was somewhat traditional, Freudian. We were cautioned about transference—taking on the symptoms of the patient."

I thought I heard a little longing in her voice, as though the idea of loving therapy had some appeal to her, yet I felt hopeless that she would be able to help me much. She seemed perplexed by my experiences and by my clear comprehension of all that was happening to me, coupled with my deep distress. She continued to ignore my questions

9

about the spiritual phenomena that had occurred for me but acknowledged that I appeared quite calm and lucid to her.

"Whatever is going on," she explained, "you'll have to stay here for several days."

"But I'm in the wrong place," I protested. "You don't understand. There's no need for me to be locked up, and I don't feel like I belong here."

She spoke more soothingly, "I don't know what's really going on with you," she said, "but you'll have to remain here for several days. It's state law. Once you're admitted to a lockup facility, you must be examined and certified by an official committee before you can be released. There's no one to do that over the weekend, so, since it's Thursday, you'll have to wait until next week."

I felt my indignation return. "I want to speak to my lawyer about this!"

10

"Of course," she responded, remaining cool, "but he will tell you the same thing." She straightened the papers on her clipboard, rose, and turned toward the door.

I glared at her back, feeling defeated. "He," I retorted, getting in the last word, "is a she."

After she left, I pondered my situation at length. I read my *Course in Miracles*. After a time, a sense of warm, serene peace seemed to come over me as I just accepted, for the moment, what was happening to me here. There was no point in fighting it. I might as well just go with it and see what lesson there was for me. I'm paying six hundred dollars a day in this place, I thought. I'm going to get any good I can out of it. I'm going to relax and rest and pray to understand all this.

I suddenly felt certain that my entire experience of the last few weeks, culminating in being locked up here, was being orchestrated by a Great Good, by God. I felt the need to just be quiet and access some great wisdom that I felt lay deep within my own tortured mind. I had always thought myself, and my life, rather ordinary, but ordinary people did not get locked up on mental wards—or did they? I wanted to think about and understand the tumultuous events of the last few weeks that had culminated in my being here. Yet I knew that wasn't enough. The roots of this had to go way back.

I realized that I needed to begin at the beginning, to review my life with brutal honesty, to look at the trials and traumas that must have led up to this crisis. Perhaps I could apply new spiritual insight to my past and heal as I did so. For though I continued to feel a small, nagging fear that I might be truly mentally ill, I had a distinct, deeper knowing that all of this was designed to reveal to me a True Way, a New Life in God. I sensed that I was in the midst of a powerful spiritual transformation.

This task of reviewing and understanding, I realized, would be an arduous and painful journey through my past. I would need a very peaceful, restful place to do it—like a hospital, perhaps? Was that why I was here? I felt up to the task, and I was ready to fulfill God's plan and purpose for me—but not tonight. I was exhausted. I let my body go limp, and my mind filled with the Light that had become so familiar and comforting to me recently. I felt myself float away into peaceful sleep for the first time in several weeks.

# TWO

# TO ALICE MILLER

*A four-year-old boy had a new baby sister. He seemed to adore her, but every day he begged his parents to be left alone with her. They were concerned, yet he was so patient and gentle with her that they finally relented. Peering through a crack in the nursery door, they watched as he approached the baby's cradle. Laying a chubby hand on her forehead, he leaned close and whispered, "Please tell me what it's like to be with God—I'm already starting to forget."*

—REVEREND MARY MANIN MORRISSEY

Friday, April 14, 1989—Early morning: I was exhilarated to have slept through the night. I had been plagued with insomnia for weeks. I got up and went to the shower room. It was huge and clean and warm, and the shower spray was fine and hard, tingling me all over. I went to the eating room for breakfast, actually feeling good to be alive. I smiled at the other patients. A few made eye contact with me, though no one smiled back.

What I noticed most about the lockup ward that morning was how quiet and peaceful it was and how simple life seemed here. There was something healing and comforting about not having anything to think about beyond my own personal needs.

I returned to my room. The morning sun was streaming in the window. I sat on my bed, and then lay back against the cool pillows that I had stacked to make a back support. It had been a long time since I had been so relaxed and worry-free—years actually. I realized that I felt a sort of freedom, like that of the unencumbered life of a child.

The thought of childhood reminded me of my intention to review my past. Somehow I knew I would have to go way back to find a time when I was truly unencumbered.

I could remember that I had been an innocent child, had known God once, but it seemed as though I had gradually begun to forget about God as I had learned from my parents to compete, to judge, and to fear. Of course, my innocent, well-intentioned parents were simply teaching me what they themselves had been taught.

Perhaps I was now being given a chance to change this deadly pattern. To do it, I believed I needed to go back and virtually reinvent myself. I needed to understand when and how it all began, then proceed to understand each stage of my development as I plunged ever more deeply into the darkness of ignorance and Godlessness.

I closed my eyes and recalled what I knew of my parents' history and how it probably had affected the family dynamics that shaped my early childhood:

In his young years, my father, Richard, was a man of attractive contrasts. He had inherited the black hair and brown eyes of the Chinook ancestors from my grandmother's side and the fair skin of my Norwegian grandfather. He was gregarious, constantly teasing to cover up his own insecurity. His mind could grasp the leading edge of technology, and he loved to cook.

When my mother, Mary Ellen, met him in Seattle in early 1943, they were both nineteen. She was slim and considered pretty with her long brown hair and clear blue eyes. With her best friend, Helen, she had fled from an unhappy home life in the Midwest. The two young women had little trouble finding jobs in wartime Seattle.

Within months after meeting, Richard and Mary Ellen were married—on June 12, 1943. I was born on June 12, 1944. For the first year of my life, my father was in Germany, serving in World War II. Returning home, he got a job that took him out of town all week. When he came home on weekends, all he wanted to do was be alone with my mother. "I resented you being there," he told me years later. I never bonded with my father, never felt truly loved by him as a child. He mostly ignored me except to criticize or tease me.

Both of my parents struggled with the effects of traumatic childhoods. My father had grown up in the shadow of an older brother whom his mother idolized. An aunt told me a story once that helped me to understand and forgive my father:

> Your father worked from the time he was very young. His older brother, Russell, was a sports hero, far too busy to work, but your dad had jobs and contributed money to the family. One time, he secretly saved a little money each week for several weeks and bought his mother a pair of slippers. It was no special occasion; he just did it to express his love. She took the slippers back to the store and used the money to buy something for Russell.

My heart ached when I thought about my mother's painful adolescent years. Her own mother died when my mother was fourteen. She describes not being allowed to cry at the funeral and going alone to her room afterwards to collect herself. No one comforted her. After the death of her mother, her father, who had always physically abused her and her siblings, began to abuse her sexually as well.

Neither of my parents ever expressed any spiritual beliefs. We simply never talked about God at all. My mother occasionally took us to church or Sunday school. I think she was troubled and searching. A grandmother she adored

15

was very pious. Deeply wounded by her childhood abuse, I think my mother believed she had to maintain a powerful, rigid mind to control the people and events of her life in order to prevent further tragedy. And I think she blamed God for the bad things that happened to her.

In the early years, after Dad returned from the war, my mother worked as a secretary to put him through college, a first in his family. He then sold his soul to the telephone company, where he tried to find happiness through material success for thirty-five years. He drowned his inevitably resulting disappointment in alcohol.

Alcohol played a major role in the social life of my parents. Every event, every family gathering was accompanied by large quantities of alcohol. There was always a stocked bar in our home. I thought that was what everybody did.

My father could build or fix anything. He was constantly working on the new house we bought every two years or so as he was transferred all over the Pacific Northwest by the phone company. He always had a beer in his hand as he did these projects. He would sometimes get into violent fights with my mother. I remember one time he lost control and put his fist through the wall. He never touched her as far as I know, but the verbal abuse, the shouting, was awful.

When I was three years old, my sister, Linda, was born. Chubby-cheeked and adorable, she was the light of my father's life. When we went to visit Grandma and Grandpa at their store, Dad's mother used to say, "Oh, Linda is such a pretty child. Why is Susie so plain?" I was jealous of Linda and abused her verbally and physically. One time I locked her in a closet and terrorized her with graphic stories of bloody monsters.

Ten years later, my parents had another daughter, Lisa, followed by a son, Keith, two years after that. More like my own babies than siblings, they were the first human beings with whom I felt truly close and loving.

There were good times in our family. We took camping trips into the gorgeous local forests. My father's sister and two remaining brothers (Russell was killed on Saipan during World War II) all loved to make music, and we always sang when we got together. I still remember dozens of old songs. I loved spending time with my aunts and uncles and all their children. Some summers Mother took us kids back to the cornfields of Illinois to visit her brothers and sisters and our cousins from her side of the family. I loved being with them, too. I always felt a deep, strong sense of family.

My mother loved me the best she knew how. She always seemed to like having me with her. She paid a lot of attention to me and took great pride in how smart and good I was, but she pushed me constantly to be a perfect little angel and always, always the smartest and the best at whatever I did. Thinking she was being a good mother, she was very strict, because that was what she was taught. I later learned that this kind of strictness is rather abusive. Though both my parents spanked us kids some, I think their verbal abuse was more frightening. I can hear my mother's words ringing in my ears: "If you don't stop crying, I'm going to smack you again. Go to your room until you can come out smiling. I'm going to slap you silly. Don't sass me back."

Striving to be perfect gravely affected my emotional life. I developed some nervous habits like nail biting—fingers and toes. In the first grade, the principal called my astounded parents into his office to inform them that I was eating away the front edge of my desk. For years, I ate paper. I ate my napkin after dinner and the ticket stubs at the theater.

A good representation of my perfectionism was my sophomore year of high school. I won medals for being the most outstanding French student and the most outstanding art student in the school as well as the top sophomore. I remember feeling a little embarrassed as no one else won more than one award that day, but mostly I felt relief and a

17

sense of satisfaction. These accomplishments were how I earned my mother's love, how I survived.

The problem was, no matter how much I excelled, I never felt good enough. I once did a pen and ink drawing for a nationwide contest. I thought it so awful that I threw it in the trash. My teacher retrieved it and submitted it, and it won first prize.

Like my father, extroverted and glib, I was quite popular—or at least widely recognized by my peers, frequently holding elective office. I always had a number of people around me though I never felt truly, deeply connected with them. I always felt alone really, always outside the "in" group.

∞

I noticed that the morning sun had moved higher, causing the shadows of the bars outside the window to stretch across my hospital bed. I felt sad thinking about how insecure I really was while growing up. I had recently done some rebirthing therapy to deal with some of my childhood issues. During one session I had gotten in touch with my abuse to my sister, Linda. Sobbing, I had called her to apologize.

I realized that I had basically been taught by my mother not to feel, that she had acknowledged only my mind, my reasoning side. Consequently, I was often unable to recognize even my deepest pain and, more importantly, totally unable to communicate it authentically to another soul. Because I could not tap into my own pain, I could not relate to or empathize with the pain of others.

I recalled reading a book by a well-known psychiatrist, Alice Miller, on the dynamics that often occur between a traumatized mother and her only, or firstborn, child—especially if that child is bright or gifted. It was called *Prisoners of Childhood: The Drama of the Gifted Child*. In it she wrote:

Quite often we are faced here with gifted patients who have been praised and admired for their talents and achievements. According to prevailing, general attitudes, these people—the pride of their parents—should have had a strong and stable sense of self-assurance. But exactly the opposite is the case. In everything they undertake they do well and often excellently; they are admired and envied; they are successful whenever they care to be—but all to no avail. Behind all this lurks depression, the feeling of emptiness and self-alienation, and a sense that their life has no meaning. . . .

One serious consequence of this early adaptation is the impossibility of experiencing certain feelings (such as jealousy, envy, anger, loneliness, impotence, anxiety) either in childhood or later in adulthood.

When I read this book, I couldn't believe how it paralleled my own life and relationship with my mother. I wrote a poem at that time about how she had manipulated me, how I could not bear to hold her accountable (because I thought that meant to blame her), and how I was healing and becoming God-conscious in spite of it.

It was paradoxical that, at the time I wrote this poem, my mother had been for several years on a healing path herself. She actually introduced me to some pivotal material that ultimately helped me to grow in spiritual awareness, yet she never really followed through to a spiritual source herself. We had been able to share a lot of painful memories from both our childhoods and heal a lot of wounds together, but I had never been able to talk to her about God.

The sun shone through the hospital window, warm on my face. I closed my eyes. I was beginning to get in touch with deep stirrings of love and compassion for the innocent child who was still alive inside me, the child who knew God intimately. The tears came as I let myself feel the pain of the lonely child I had become as I forgot Him.

19

## TO ALICE MILLER

A child moulded to a perfect pitch,
Squeezing the soft brain clay,
Sculpting a form out of razor sharp
Perception,
Is a child
Who cowers and quivers in
Desperate ambivalence.

It is unbearable to attack the womb.
To think of destroying the physical place
Of conception
Is to deny one's existence.
The resulting spiritual wasteland,
Is a living Death.

For love does not happen.
The entire class is full of hated and
Hateful persons.
If I am best, THEY will take on
The ambivalence.
They will hate me
And love me
Out of grudging respect.

It is true, Alice.
I went to the zoo.
The penguin skeleton and
The eagle skeleton are so like mine.
I am no better than the penguin.
Oh me, god.
I am the penguin.

SUSAN BREWSTER

JULY 1986

20

# JANE'S PAIN

*The Holy Spirit promotes healing by looking beyond it to
what the children of God were before healing was needed,
and will be when they have been healed.*

—*A Course in Miracles* (5.II.1:2)

Friday, April 14, 1989—Afternoon: Lunch was better
than dinner the night before, or maybe I was just tasting things with a different tongue. An hour or so after eating a hot turkey sandwich with stuffing and cranberry
sauce, I was summoned to exercise group. Because I had
been experiencing anxiety, I was not allowed to do anything
more rigorous than make slow circles with my arms.

When I returned to my room, I was surprised to see
that I had gotten a roommate. She was sitting on the edge
of her bed, just staring at nothing. I sat down on my bed
and looked at her. She was very young, late teens or early
twenties. Her face caused my heart to jump. It was swollen
and bruised and she had bandages around her head and
both wrists.

"Hello, I'm Susan," I said softly. "What happened to
you?"

"I fell. I'm fine now. I wish they would let me go home.
My dog is all alone. I love her so much. She needs me."

She spoke in a dull monotone, but I could sense the
pain in her voice. She told me she had "spells" when she
would faint and fall and hurt herself. I knew there were no

doubt other things going on for her, or else she wouldn't be here. I was certain the wrist bandages meant she had attempted suicide. Her name was Margaret.

I felt some mystical energy move very deep inside me. It seemed to come from the core of my heart. Focusing on it, I realized it felt faintly familiar, like I had felt it long ago. It seemed to have to do with Margaret and her dog and her suicide attempt, but I couldn't quite make the connection.

Margaret lay down on her bed and was soon snoring softly. I was glad to see her relieved of her pain for now. Though my heart had been opening slowly in the past months, it was still rare for me to feel such deep, genuine empathy and concern for someone. My ability to feel seemed to be increasing even more rapidly here. I was excited at this prospect but fearful too. If I had repressed as much pain and rage as I thought I had all my life, I could be opening a Pandora's box.

22

I remembered being extremely sensitive when I was very young. I knew there had been relationships and events in my childhood that had affected me deeply. Exactly when had I begun to repress my feelings? I had learned from my parents that it was bad to express my pain and fear and especially my anger. I had to pretend that they didn't matter. To heal this behavior, I realized I needed to recall actual incidents.

As I thought about this, a scene from my sixth grade year came into clear, vivid focus and would not go away. I lay back against the pillows, closed my eyes, and recalled a specific morning in September 1956:

∞

"I get to share this desk with you."

I stared up at the new girl. At twelve, she was already a beauty, tall and lissome. She had blue-green eyes and a strong chin with a cleft. Round patches of rich color seemed to have been scrubbed into her cheeks. Not exactly pink, they were more like a warm red.

"What's your name?" I asked her.

"Jane Stanley," she said. "My parents call me Janey," she added, "but I prefer to be called Jane." I was impressed by her assertiveness. She reminded me of me.

I held out my hand. "Sue, not Susie," I laughed. From that day forward, we sat together, wrote romance novels together, slept, ate, and talked endlessly together.

One day, I came to school to find Jane waiting for me in the back of the room, her coat still on.

"Where have you been?" she hissed. "I have something for you."

She opened her coat. Nestled against her was a tiny black kitten. "I found it on the way to school. My dad's allergic. There's no way I can keep it. Do you think your mom would let you have it, and it could sort of be mine, too?" Her eyes beseeched me anxiously.

"I don't know, but I'll ask," I whispered back. I was doubtful.

To my surprise, my parents let me keep the kitten. I named her Coalbin. I was enchanted by her antics as a young kitten, but as she became a mature cat, I grew to love her more than any other being in my life. I would lie on my bed with my arm around her, bury my face in her warm, clean-smelling fur, and tell her all my secret sorrows.

She replaced my teddy bear, Goo Goo, whom I had worn out with caressing, and my imaginary playmate, Robin, whom my mother insisted I give up because I was "too old for such things," as the only spiritual relationship in my early life. They were my confidants, my only givers of unconditional love, my angels. Jane was a constant companion and we loved each other, but we had no idea how to express it. Who would have taught us? Her parents did not know their God selves any more than mine did.

23

When school was out for that summer, Jane and I continued to bike to each other's houses every day. One day she called me shrieking, "We're going to Yellowstone Park, and my folks said you can come!"

I had a wonderful vacation with the Stanleys, but I missed Coalbin desperately. On our return, as soon as they dropped me off in my driveway, I whizzed past my waiting parents and began tearing all around the yard calling, "Kitty, kitty!" I whipped through the house, then back out to them. "I can't find her," I wailed, pausing to ask for assistance. Suddenly, I noticed their faces. They looked confused.

"We took her to the pound, Dear," my mother said slowly. "The fleas were biting your father something awful, and he couldn't stand it any more."

I didn't know what the pound was, but I instinctively knew something catastrophic had occurred. "What are you talking about?!" I said, my voice raising to a scream. "We have to go get her right now!"

My mother spoke with her usual unapproachable authority, but I noticed she kept glancing nervously at my father. "I'm afraid that's impossible, Susie. She's been put to sleep."

I stared at them frantically. Finally comprehending, I ran into the house, into my empty room, and slammed the door. I sobbed for several hours, coming out only once for Kleenex.

After a time, my mother came to the door. "Susie, I had no idea you would feel this bad," she said.

How could you know? I thought dully. You have no idea how I feel about anything. What you mean is, "I had no idea you would ever have the courage to express so much pain. I thought I taught you better." I had been trained by her to shut down my pain, my frustration, my fury, my fear. It was to be years before I unlocked the rage I felt at my mother that day, years before I was able to access the pain enough to express it to another human being.

I was unable to verbalize my grief and anger even to Jane. We still retained some inborn ability to empathize, she and I, but mostly our parents, themselves completely hardened, had succeeded in hardening us as well. She did tell me often that she hated her father, but we had no idea how to really talk about these things. The closest we came to real intimacy was to make a pact to stick together and to never be like our mean parents.

∞

Margaret still slept soundly in the bed across the room. It was a peaceful afternoon on the lockup ward. I found the quiet very soothing as old wounds were opened up.

We had a bathroom with a commode and sink in our room. I got up and went to the bathroom. I heard Margaret stir on her bed, groaning pitifully. I wanted desperately to know how to make her more comfortable. I realized that my feelings of concern and compassion suddenly seemed almost overwhelming.

25

I returned to my bed and relaxed against the pillows. I found myself wondering why Margaret had tried to take her own life. For no apparent reason, this question began to echo repeatedly through my mind. Moreover, it felt familiar, like I had asked it before about someone else. I realized that to complete my understanding of how I repressed pain, I needed to jump ahead in time, to complete the saga of Jane. There was something pivotal in my relationship with her in my awakening to my true, feeling Self.

∞

Jane and I saw each other only periodically after sixth grade as we headed off to different schools, but we always maintained our special heart connection. After high school, Jane got a master's degree and married her history professor, Charles Briggs. They had two little boys. We wrote some letters. She seemed happy.

She began working as a reporter for a Seattle television station in the seventies, eventually becoming a substitute news anchor. I visited her every so often, and we caught up on all our secrets—just like the old days. On one visit, she took me on a tour of the TV studio. On the way home we stopped at a Safeway store. People kept walking up to her. "Aren't you Jane Briggs?" they would ask excitedly.

We spent several hours reminiscing in the living room of her charming older home. She was more beautiful than ever: blonde hair, still slim and stately. I admired the large bouquet of red roses on the dining room table. "Charles brings me roses every night," she said, smiling.

My next trip to Seattle was a few months later. I called Jane and was amazed to find her number disconnected. I called her parents. Her mother told me Jane had left Charles and moved to Texas with the boys. She had taken a position as a news anchor with a TV station there. I was shocked. I got her address and planned to write, but I was terribly busy with four little children and kept putting it off.

A few months later, I again visited Seattle. On this trip, I spent time with some other girlfriends from high school. On a kick, we decided to go see our old neighborhood. We were wild with excitement and mirth as we visited favorite haunts and remembered our many adventures.

As we approached a familiar corner, I exclaimed, "Hey, this is Janey Stanley's old street. Let's go by her house. Has anyone heard how she's doing?"

Everyone froze. After what felt like hours, my friend, Charmien, said, "My God, Sue, haven't you heard? Don't you of all people know? Jane committed suicide in Texas a couple of weeks ago. She shut herself in her car in the garage. It was in all the papers."

∞

I kept my eyes closed for several minutes, typically fighting the feelings evoked by this memory of Jane's suicide. I recalled that I had not cried about it at the time, but I had felt that same energy deep in my heart that I had felt when I first saw my new roommate, Margaret, earlier that afternoon. I opened my eyes and looked frantically for something on which to focus them. I stared at the flowered pattern that tumbled across the legs of my favorite cotton pants outfit—the outfit I was wearing at the time and the only clothing I had brought to the hospital.

Suddenly, I felt something snap inside me. I was overcome with pure, unstoppable grief. I got up and went into the bathroom and gathered a huge wad of toilet paper. Returning to my bed, I let myself cry for a long time.

Margaret, awake now, just sat and watched me. "Why are you crying, Susan?" she finally asked. Her voice was sad and concerned.

"I was just thinking about some old friends who died. You would have loved one of them," I sobbed. "She was a beautiful black cat named Coalbin."

"Oh," she said, "I know what you mean. I really miss my dog terribly." Her face mirrored my sorrow.

When I felt completely drained of pain, I looked at her again. "I never got to say good-bye," I sighed, "and I didn't even know how to tell them that I loved them."

"I really miss my dog," she repeated. As I looked at her, I was aware of a strange feeling. I realized it was love.

Two attendants, a doctor, and a nurse came and took Margaret away shortly after that. I wondered where they were taking her. "Where are you taking her?" I asked, but they all ignored me.

As she trudged by my bed, flanked by the two husky attendants, she looked back at me. "Good-bye, Susan," she said softly.

"Good-bye, Margaret," I answered. I wanted to add, "I love you," but my reason kicked in and stopped me. How, it asked, could I possibly love someone I had only known for a couple of hours?

I lay back on my bed against the pillows. This was becoming my pondering position. I thought about Margaret's pain—pain so great that she literally couldn't bear it. I thought about Jane's pain and its identical effect. I thought about pain and I thought about death. This was difficult for me, because whenever I had thought about death, ever since I was a little girl, I felt like I was falling into a deep, dark spiral of terror. My conscious thought was always: My God, someday I am going to cease to exist. I would immediately force myself to stop thinking about it, because I would feel as though I were becoming overwhelmed with fear.

I realized that this was more of my pattern of denial of feelings. Early in life, I had adopted a fundamental belief that it was absolutely unacceptable to feel any negative feelings like pain and grief and fear. This was most obvious in major incidents like the deaths of Coalbin and Jane, but it also infiltrated every aspect of my life. Moreover, I was consequently never really able to fully express my positive feelings such as joy, compassion, or love.

I could see that something was happening here in the hospital to change that pattern. God was helping me see it, and Margaret had been an angel who came to teach it to me. I missed Margaret already.

# FOUR

# MUTINY

*The truth in you remains as radiant as a star, as pure as light, as innocent as love itself.*

—*A Course in Miracles* (31.VI.7:4)

Friday, April 14, 1989—Evening: At last the warm, kindly nurse of my fantasies appeared at the door of my hospital room. "How are we doing, Dear?" she asked. Her tone was soft, concerned.

I was taking a medication called Xanax for my anxiety. I asked her whether it was time for another dose. "You just go down there to the nurses' station for your meds, Hon, whenever you need some," she said. I felt almost adult, almost trusted, almost in control of my own life again.

I looked into the nurse's twinkling blue eyes. "Can I visit with the other patients?" I asked her. I felt a strange, deep longing to connect with and understand the people here.

She frowned slightly. "No, Dear, we discourage that."

"But why?" I asked.

She looked at me for several moments. "Well, you seem different," she began, "but many of the patients here don't know how to interact appropriately. Sometimes there's unwanted touching, and that can lead to problems."

She got up. "I'm going to get some supplies for you." She smiled, calling back over her shoulder, "I'll be back in a bit."

After she left, I lay back on my bed to rest. The room was very quiet. I loved having nowhere to go, no one to see, nothing to do. It was a blissful state that I later learned to create consciously in my life.

I thought about what the nice nurse had said: "Sometimes there is unwanted touching, and that can lead to problems." The words had a familiar ring. My mother had said a very similar phrase to me, more than once, many years before.

I knew sexuality had played a major role in my emotional development in spite of my mother's attempt to downplay it. I had understood her fears better when I had become the mother of daughters myself, suddenly realizing why mothers are concerned that their daughters will discover the delights of sex and become pregnant before it is time. Moreover, I realized there had still been a strong residue of Victorian and Christian sexual repression in the culture in my developing years. My parents were not the only ones who did not discuss sex freely with their children.

In addition to these normal concerns and repressions, however, I believed my mother saw in my developing sexuality the loss of my perfection, my precious innocence, and worse, my absolute loyalty to her alone. She also, I thought, had a basic distrust of men and their sexual aggression, probably because of her sexual abuse.

She had basically ignored my sexual feelings and tried to teach me to do the same, but feelings as powerful as my sexual feelings could be repressed for only so long. So with no guidance from my parents and no spiritual guidance, I was left to flounder helplessly in the vast sea of passionate confusion that was my adolescent sexuality. I had no idea how sex fit into a loving relationship. Indeed, I had never even observed a healthy, loving relationship.

I realized that this dilemma of my sexuality had contributed to my dark ignorance and my ever-widening separation from God. This, then, was the next part of my life that needed examining. I closed my eyes and recalled my early childhood sexual experiences, my subsequent repression, and my first year of college—when I had finally, reluctantly, allowed myself overt sexual expression.

∞

I could remember feeling very sexual as a young child. I played doctor with my sister and friends and fantasized about movie and television heroes.

When I was about nine, my mother began to lecture me on the evils of sex "at the wrong time, in the wrong place, with the wrong person." I could see nothing right about it from her standpoint, so I simply tried to forget about it. My high school nickname was Miss Frigidaire.

Though I tried, I could not keep hot passion from possessing my mind and body. I obsessed, and I masturbated, shinnying up poles or on the side of the bathtub, frequently and secretly. I never knew that's what it was called or that the ecstatic result was an orgasm. I didn't make the connection until after two years of married, non-orgasmic sex.

I was outgoing and funny as a girl. I was a little chubby but had a cute, chesty figure and a bright smile. Boys liked me, and I always had a boyfriend. I loved to neck, but I knew absolutely where my mother expected me to draw the line. Necking meant kissing and holding hands—period.

My father was transferred to the East Coast in 1962, the year I graduated from high school. My parents decided, despite years of promises, that there was not enough money for me to go away to college. So I lived at home and went to a small, local liberal arts university. I remembered feeling bitterly disappointed.

It was about this time that I began to rebel against my mother's strict dogma. To many, my rebellion must have seemed so mild as to have been laughable, but one must keep in mind the context of purity and perfection from

31

which I was straying. I equated being sexual with being positively evil and degenerate. I remembered my freshman year of college and the end of my sexual innocence:

September 1962: Marla Epstein pressed her hand over her mouth to keep from laughing and regarded me with a patronizing, sympathetic look. "It takes a few times, Sue," she soothed. "You'll get it. You're doing great."

Feeling woozy and weak, I sank down onto the edge of her bed, one of two in the tiny dorm room, and regarded her skeptically. Through the blue smoke haze from the smoldering menthol cigarette that protruded awkwardly from between my two extended fingers, I looked at her admiringly.

She was about my height, five foot four or five, with a centerfold figure. She was softly, smoothly brown all over. She had light brown skin, long brown hair and big, warm brown eyes edged with thick lashes and topped with high arched brows. Her nose was small and roundish, her mouth full-lipped and sensual. She exuded sexuality in a sort of earthy, smoke-soaked, cocky way, but there were dark circles under her eyes, and she looked run-down and a bit disheveled.

Nevertheless, I felt like a pale, naive dumpling child next to her. I was determined to emulate this powerful, fast-speaking girl from Brooklyn—wherever that was. And I longed to be, or at least appear to be, Jewish too—whatever that was.

Marla, seemingly outgoing and confident, was nonetheless a lonely new freshman like myself. She had a good heart, but she was manipulative and self-absorbed. She found in me a convenient friend. I was happy to be wanted in this strange, new environment.

We pushed our one-piece desk/seats together in the back of the huge botany lecture class we both attended, and Marla launched what she considered my most truly vital education; she lectured me endlessly about sex: "I can't believe you've never done it," she hissed. "I'm sixteen and I've been doing it for years."

I was flabbergasted. "But, how can you be sixteen and be in college?" I asked. I was blushing as I ignored the more sensitive reference.

"I skipped," she said. She raised one dark eyebrow dramatically. "You know," she whispered, looking around to be sure no one was eavesdropping, "I think I might be pregnant." She looked far from concerned, seeming pleased with my little gasp of dismay.

I clucked sympathetically. "What are you going to do?" I asked.

"Oh, I'll just get rid of it. My family knows doctors." She pulled a lipstick out of her purse and began applying it. I noticed that her fingernails were bitten well down below the quick, belying her casualness. I felt compassion for her, mixed with admiration for her chutzpah.

"You know, Sue, you really can't stay a virgin. We have to do something about this." She looked directly into my eyes and smiled wickedly.

"Well, I don't know," I said, beginning to feel a familiar discomfort. All the years of my mother's pleadings and warnings were resounding in my ears as my hormones danced at the very thought.

"I'll take you to Princeton," she pronounced resolutely, as though that would fix everything.

Several days later, as we whispered and passed notes throughout another botany lecture, she confided that she had started her period and that her friend, Neil, a sophomore at Princeton, shared a suite with three other guys, and they were expecting us the weekend after next. I was apprehensive but excited. Princeton was Ivy League. Even a girl from out West knew what that meant. I didn't know if I was ready to be deflowered there, but I looked forward to experiencing Princeton—and Princeton boys.

33

Our campus was lovely with its old colonial, white-pillared brick buildings, but I have never seen a more charming and gorgeous place than Princeton was that fall. Having grown up in modern West Coast suburbs, I was utterly enchanted. Most of the buildings at Princeton were huge and very old, their stone edifices almost completely covered with ivy. They reminded me of European castles and cathedrals, dark and dignified and strangely inviting. All the buildings were surrounded with lush lawns, trees, pachysandra beds, and shrubbery. Brick or cobblestone paths curved gracefully around them.

The weather that weekend was sunny and crisp, and the memory-evoking smell of smoldering leaf piles permeated the air. The bells chimed from the stone tower of the old campus church. The dining hall, huge and warm, echoed with the shouts and laughter of hundreds of privileged boys and their weekend girlfriends.

34

We met Neil and his roommates in the dining hall. They were all attractive and full of fun and, of course, very bright. A tall, slim, dark-haired fellow with horn-rimmed glasses claimed me immediately. His name was Mike. I, of course, was attracted to a bulkier specimen with a blond crew cut. He mostly ignored me as I pined for him, always feeling that I was with the wrong guy.

After lunch, we all gathered in the fellows' apartment. Bottles of beer were distributed, and everyone settled into deep couches and big, soft chairs to get acquainted.

"Do you want to go to the football game this afternoon?" Mike asked me.

"Oh, yes," I cried. "I love football." I did.

I noticed that Neil and Marla made no move to join us an hour later as we left for the stadium. Mike bought me a black and orange striped muffler that I treasured for years, and we screamed ourselves hoarse as the Princeton team soundly trounced Yale.

"Where is Marla?" I asked a roommate when we returned.

"Oh, she and Neil are in his bedroom," he said, winking at me knowingly. "They'll be in there all weekend." I pretended I didn't understand and quickly changed the subject.

The enchantment of that weekend grew for me as we attended a dance that night. I stood at a grand piano watching a young man who jumped and screamed and gyrated and pounded the keyboard until I was positive the piano wouldn't survive. His name was Jerry Lee Lewis.

I knew how to convey nonverbal hands-off messages, and I did so for the remainder of the weekend. It wasn't so much that I didn't want to be more physically intimate as that it was a deeply ingrained habit to put it off. Mike seemed equally inexperienced, so we successfully avoided and mutually denied our longings through that and two more weekends, at which point Marla gave up.

On Monday, Marla and I returned to the studies that we were having increasing difficulty taking very seriously. I found some pleasure in an art history class with Mrs. Kosinski, a tiny, somewhat shriveled old woman with a heavy European accent. She had bright orange hair wisping around her elfin face and pulled into a little bun high on her head.

"Today, vee vill study zee vonderful pentings of Van Gock," she chirped.

I enjoyed the studio even more, but mostly I was caught up in the kaleidoscopic melee that was eastern college social life. There were dances and parties and bonfires, and it was all so new and exciting to me. My studies suffered enormously, and letters of the alphabet appeared on my grade reports that I had never seen before. I cared, but it was not nearly as important to me as being socially accepted and liked.

Marla was dating several boys at school. She kept encouraging and coaching me in womanly wiles and trying to set me up with someone whom I couldn't resist. I wasn't unwilling, just scared.

One night, I met her on campus for a required evening lecture on exotic flowering trees. Outside the hall, she suddenly grabbed my arm and said, "Do you want to do something a lot more fun than this?"

"Marla," I protested, "I've got to bring my grades up. My parents are having fits."

"Oh, come on," she grinned, "this is going to be so boring. I have an idea for some real fun."

I wavered.

"It involves some real cute boys," she taunted.

I fell.

She was very mysterious as we slipped out of line and headed for the student union.

36

"Give me a minute," she said, pulling a dime from her purse. She walked over to a pay phone and dialed, chatted briefly, then returned to me, smiling like a cartoon character.

"It's all set," she said.

"What's all set?" I asked. I was curious but suspicious.

"We're going to go visit Bob and Tom and Gary," she announced. She giggled and raised her eyebrow, waiting for my reaction.

"What are you talking about?" I asked, trying to keep the hysteria out of my voice. "They live in the boys' dorm. We can't go in there, Marla!"

"Oh God, Sue, don't be such a child. I do it all the time."

After several more minutes of coaxing, I found myself following her reluctantly toward the far corner of the campus where the freshmen boys' dorm stood in a grove of now bare maple trees. It was a cloudless night, misty and cold. A quarter moon wanly lit the landscape, but it seemed as bright as midday to me. As we approached the two-story brick dorm, I could see lights on in nearly every window and hear the sounds of deep boy shouts coming through them, even though they were all closed tight against the damp, cold night. I could feel my heart thudding in my chest.

"Marla," I hissed, "I don't want to do this."

"Sssshhh," she laid her index finger on her lips, frowned ferociously, and glared at me.

We reached the dorm and slipped silently through a back door that was opened for us by someone who apparently was waiting for us inside. It was very dark everywhere. Tripping over the first step, I followed Marla and the mystery man up a flight of stairs, and we emerged into brightly lit bedlam. We passed quickly down the hall to hoots and whistles and in the door of a room containing four bunks, desks, chairs, and I'm not sure what else because everything was buried in dirty underwear, soggy towels, and soccer gear.

It is hard to convey today how terrifying an experience this was for me. The Victorian morals of just thirty years ago have been so totally revised that we now find such adventures merely amusing, but at that time, in that place, I felt like a criminal who had entered a bank to steal a million dollars.

Gradually, I relaxed. The boys were successfully hiding any apprehension they might have felt with loud bravado and humor. Out came the inevitable beer. We all lit up cigarettes and proceeded to chat and laugh and dance to rock-and-roll music for several hours. By about ten o'clock, I had completely forgotten where I was and was having the time of my life. A couple of other boys had joined us, and Marla and I were the center of much admiring attention and excitement.

Suddenly, there were loud thuds on the closed door of the room, and a deep male voice roared over the din, "Open up, you guys, I know you have girls in there!"

"In the closet," Bob whispered frantically.

We didn't pause to argue. As quickly and quietly as we could, we slipped into the dark recesses of the closet as Tom held the door for us, closing it silently behind us. With the darkness, the pungent odor of the closet, the effects of the beer, and my terror, I thought for sure I was going to faint. I felt Marla's arm around my waist, and I returned the hug. As we clung to each other there in the blackness, I realized that she was silently saying how sorry she was.

Marla was suspended for the rest of the term. Because I was a commuter, I escaped similar punishment—but we both had to endure an hour with Mrs. Livermore. Mrs. Livermore, the Dean of Women, was about ninety-something. She looked like anyone's grandmother, only she stood like Napoleon and was about as cheerful. She wore steel-rimmed spectacles, which did not hide her piercing, steely blue eyes.

Mrs. Livermore had reputedly never been known to embrace either understanding or forgiveness. She governed the women's student body with absolute ruthlessness, demanding obedience of all rules. She felt it her personal responsibility to see that all the young women were not just educated but remained vestal virgins. I'm sure my mother thought she was terrific.

I missed Marla terribly. Thankfully there were only three weeks left of the semester. When she returned, we swore we were going to be very good for the remainder of the year. Indeed we became quite subdued, but nothing short of solitary confinement could have stopped us from our giggling secrets about—and our pursuit of—*boys*.

At a spring dance, I met a young man I liked. He was a visitor, but I was impressed that he seemed to know all the upperclassmen. He was smallish but stocky, and I was attracted to his green eyes, blond hair, and impish grin. His name was Bob Brewster. Little did I know he was to be the father of my children.

"How come you know everyone?" I asked him.

"I used to go here," he explained. "I got kicked out for burning the Dean of Women in effigy."

"Oh my God, really?" I gasped. "What does that mean?"

"The old bitch is insane. She was always making trouble for us all, so we got drunk one night and made a dummy and put a sign around it with her name on it and hung it in a tree. Then we set fire to it, and . . . we got caught," he finished. He shrugged, looking at me with a sheepish grin.

I told him of my recent adventure. We became retrospective partners in crime—and future partners in life. It became known that I was his woman, that we were a couple—Bob and Sue. Marla was delighted that I was thus enmeshed and checked in daily to see if we had properly consummated our romance.

Bob was no less eagerly and similarly intentioned. Longing for the approval of the two of them, I tried my best to overcome my long-standing, carefully protected frigidity. I finally capitulated one day in the back seat of my '54 Ford.

I was profoundly suffused with guilt and regret by the end of my year at college. Bob and I had begun sneaking sex regularly, and we both believed it was bad and we were bad. I remember our being horrified when my period was late.

I never saw Marla again after that year. I left school and went to work, marrying Bob two years later.

The nice nurse returned, interrupting my reverie. "I've brought you some clean sheets and towels, Dear. Let me know if you need anything else." I thanked her and she bustled out.

I lay back on the pillows and thought about how that year at college had changed my life. I realized that I was still struggling to understand the meaning of truly healthy sexuality. After that year, I had tried desperately to atone for

39

what I saw as my fall from grace by dutifully following traditional cultural patterns of work, marriage, and children. I had felt morally obligated to marry Bob. But no matter what I did, I was never able to restore in my own mind my state of naive perfection, the one instilled by my mother.

Becoming aware of what I assumed to be my natural human propensity for sin, I had inwardly plunged into a long-lived state of self-doubt and self-recrimination. This prevented me from discovering a sense of true purpose in my life. I continued to forget about God. I had no conduit to love and the true happiness of intimate relationship and selfless service—except through motherhood.

I got up and put clean sheets on my bed, then I went up to the nurses' station and asked for meds. I returned to my room, took my meds, then took my second shower of the day, drying with the clean towel the nice nurse had brought me. Crawling into bed, I read my *Course in Miracles*, trying to calm my thoughts and get ready for sleep. Maybe God will help me to understand this issue of sexuality, I thought. I felt a peaceful feeling come over me, a sense of something wonderful. I realized it was the recognition of my own enduring, eternal innocence.

# FIVE

# BOB AND SUE

*And the Lord God said, It is not good that the man should be alone; I will make him a helper fit for him.*

—GENESIS 2:18

S aturday, April 15, 1989—Morning: My first visitor was my son, Leigh, who came charging into my room like an enraged bull elephant. "Mom! What the hell happened? I drove up here as soon as I could! They told me you might be suicidal! What the hell is going on, Mom?!"

I looked at his red face and snapping blue eyes—Leigh had never been a calm child. I knew his outburst was caused by extreme frustration, fear, and embarrassment. I remembered feeling exactly the same way twenty-four hours ago.

At twenty-two, Leigh was still my curly-headed, irrepressible boy. He was bright, loving, and full of fun. He was also impatient and hot-tempered. I adored him as I did all four of my children. He was a junior at the university, two hours south of town.

I hugged him, surprised that he was still growing. I hadn't seen him in over a month, though I had talked to him frequently. I had become concerned as he had changed from a slim child to a husky adolescent at about age twelve, but now he was becoming a man, taller and more muscular.

I asked him to sit down, then addressed his questions, realizing that in the midst of my own distress, I still needed to be the nurturing mother. "I don't know for sure what is going on, Hon. You remember I've been seeing Jack again?"

Leigh nodded. "You told me."

"Well, he and I had gone down to Grampa's on Wednesday. You know how sick I've been, how bizarre I've been feeling?"

"Uh-huh, I know, Mom," Leigh replied.

"Well, I just completely lost it that day. I entered another reality in a way. I could relate to people and things around me, but I was in a strange world of Light and Peace. I guess Grampa was pretty upset."

"Yeah, I talked to him," Leigh said.

I didn't want to talk about my father right now. I went on, "Jack dropped me home about midnight. I couldn't sleep again, and I just started feeling like I couldn't go on. But I certainly never considered suicide as a solution—my fear that I was dying was the problem!"

"So you weren't suicidal?"

"No way, Leigh. I knew I had to get some serious help, so I called Dr. Ryan, my regular doctor, in the middle of the night, even though I hadn't seen her for this and she didn't know what was going on. I told her I felt I needed to go to a hospital, that I felt like I was dying, but I didn't mean a mental hospital."

"Guess you should have been more specific, Mom," Leigh said with a little amused grunt. I could tell he was beginning to relax.

I smiled, then continued, "I just knew I needed some peace and rest. I didn't know where else to go. Dr. Ryan must have assumed then that I was suicidal. She told me Grampa had called her that night too, convinced I was on drugs or some stupid thing. They just didn't understand."

Leigh stared at me for a moment, then ran his spread fingers through his curly hair. "My God, Mom, I don't know what to believe or think. I just want you to be OK. Everyone is really upset and worried about you, even Dad."

"Really?" I said. I was surprised. Bob and I had been divorced for several years. "What did your dad say?"

"He was just really concerned. He seemed shocked. None of us had any idea it was this bad, Mom."

I thought about how it must seem to my children. If I had felt devastated at the realization of where I was and what it meant, what did they all think and feel about their mother being locked up on a mental ward? Perhaps they were even feeling fear about their own sanity, remembering reports of mental illness being hereditary.

I tried again to reassure my worried son. "Well, I truly am in the wrong place, Leigh. I've learned there is another psych ward here that's not a lockup ward, but apparently they brought me here because they assumed I was suicidal. Once you're here, you have to stay until they test you or something, which they can't do till next week."

"You have to stay here a week?"

"Yes. I think I can rest here as well as anywhere though." I thought a moment, then added carefully, "Besides, sometimes I do wonder just a little about my mental state. A lot of strange things have been happening to me. I believe they are spiritual in some way, but no one seems to understand. No one here seems to know how to explain it or help me with it. They treated me horribly when I came in. They gave me some awful drug."

"Well, you seem OK to me now."

"I feel quite a bit better, yet sometimes I wonder why I'm really here. I have questions still unanswered." I reached out and squeezed my son's arm. "Regardless, I'm going to make the best of it because I do have to stay here for a few days. I really want to see everyone. Please tell them all to come and visit me."

We talked for an hour or so. Leigh seemed convinced that I was at least sane and at peace when he left. I felt much better knowing he would convey this to the rest of the family. As a matter of fact, his visit had allayed a little secret fear

43

that had been nagging at me—that everyone would be too ashamed and afraid to come and see me.

After he had gone, I sat on the edge of my bed and reflected on his visit. I had really enjoyed seeing him. It reminded me that there was still a different world outside. How quickly I had adapted to a totally new environment.

Something Leigh had said was really sticking with me. I lay back on the bed to think. My thoughts kept focusing on how he had told me that my ex-husband, Bob, was concerned about me. Bob, bitter and deeply hurt about our divorce, had alienated himself from me for thirteen years.

My mind brought up pictures of our marriage. I could see how it had definitely been a factor in what I was beginning to see as my gradual descent into a state of deeply hidden confusion and darkness in my life. I had tried to do marriage and kids perfectly, like everything else, but no matter what I did, I couldn't create happiness with Bob.

I recognized that this was another significant event in my story, something else that needed healing. I closed my eyes and recalled this time of my life, beginning on my wedding day, nearly twenty-five years ago.

∞

For our wedding on July 25, 1965, I made my own wedding dress of beautiful Swiss cotton lace. I experienced The Day as a glorious dream—having little to do with Bob. My deep inner knowing was that our relationship was based on roles that we were both playing because we were supposed to. We had no idea how to communicate, and we had no clue about how to love one another.

We moved into a brand new apartment in New Jersey, and Bob began a career in computer sales. Shortly thereafter, the letter that every young man of the Vietnam era dreaded came in the mail: Bob was called to serve in the Army. He applied to Officer Candidate School (OCS) at Fort Benning in Georgia and was accepted.

Another determined New Jersey Army wife, Judy Olivo, and I moved to Fort Benning to be with our husbands. Wives were most unwelcome at OCS. The saying was "If the Army had wanted you to have a wife they would have issued you one." The only time we were officially permitted to see the guys was on Sundays at church. It was the talk of the company when I became pregnant. On Sunday mornings, Judy and I would prepare a gourmet breakfast in a cooler and wait for our beloveds in the parking lot. They would sneak into the back seat of her 1962 Impala convertible and hide on the floor. Judy would drive cautiously out to the Georgia woods where the four of us would picnic and make love.

The happy, welcome result of this rebellious behavior was our first child—a son, Leigh. I flew home to New Jersey to have Leigh. It was an easy birth. My doctor was skilled at administering an anaesthetic procedure known as a caudal. "Only twenty percent of women have an opening in the caudal canal located at the base of the tailbone," he told me. "We will be able to insert a tiny tube and inject anaesthetic into your spinal column constantly throughout hard labor and delivery. You will feel nothing." I happily watched the whole thing on a TV screen like it was happening to someone else. However, I experienced the full emotional impact of this miracle of birth.

Leigh was a colicky baby who cried for the first three months of his life. He developed great lungs, but it was tough on his frantic parents. In desperation, we gave him a pacifier coated with honey. I think he must have ingested many quarts of honey as a tiny infant. Trying to calm his crying, Bob rocked him so hard in the rocking chair one time that it went right over backwards. Nevertheless, we thought Leigh was the smartest, cutest baby who ever lived.

The Vietnam War was at its peak at this time. Half of Bob's OCS class—all infantry second lieutenants—were killed in Vietnam. We were lucky. The day Bob graduated

45

from OCS, he was astute (or terrified) enough to garner a spot in the Military Police. We spent his two-year tour at a post in Washington State.

Our daughter, Jaqui, was born there in the military hospital, in the military way. Spoiled by Leigh's birth, I was traumatized by having to have this baby with no anaesthetic and no preparation for natural childbirth. We new army mothers were up and around, making our own beds, a few hours after delivering. We stood in line to get our babies, then sat in rows of hard chairs to nurse them.

It was all worth it, however; I was thrilled to share my birthday, June 12, with my first daughter. My water broke in the early morning of June 11 and, to the doctor's amazement, I purposely waited until after midnight to have her. She was tiny (about five pounds), feisty, and stubborn from day one. She remained tiny, feisty, and stubborn all her life. Throughout her childhood, we sparred constantly, yet I adored her.

We returned to New Jersey after Bob's discharge and built a new little house in a subdivision in the country. There we made two more babies. Thankfully, I had my caudal doctor for both.

When Erik, my third child, was just born, I looked over at him and knew immediately that there was something special about him. He never uttered a peep, just looked all around at his big bright new world, flashing two deep dimples. His nature remained sunny throughout early childhood. Frequently giving big slobbery kisses to everyone, including all our many pets, he was a born lover of all.

My fourth pregnancy was a shock: I became pregnant while menstruating. Yet Libbi was to be the child who inherited my own artistic temperament, and we spent many hours in happy unison. She was, however, a tomboy—rejecting dresses and dolls, playing army and cowboys for endless hours with her brother, Erik, with whom she formed a very close bond. I tried in vain to put her in frills.

Years later she was able to acknowledge that she was gay. Then I understood.

At one point, all four children were under five years old. How I loved them. I remembered those years as an ecstatic blur of birthing, breast-feeding, rocking, cooing, and nuzzling. I thought babies were the most precious creatures on earth. Those times with my babies were the only experience of deep, unconditional love I was to have for a number of years.

Bob and I continued to follow our scripts in a sort of passionless play. We moved to Seattle in 1973. After fixing up a huge, modern house there, we decided we needed a new project. We began looking for the proverbial old farmhouse on a few acres. Our search extended to Oregon, where we eventually acquired a huge, dilapidated but picturesque Victorian farmhouse on sixty acres.

Here we acted out the final chapter of our marriage. Libbi, Erik, Jaqui, and Leigh were three, five, seven, and eight, respectively, when we moved to the farm. We bought horses and cows and chickens and sheep and pigs and cats and dogs and a rubber boa constrictor named Bela la Boa. I learned to slop hogs, saddle ponies, plant corn, drive an old John Deere tractor, round up runaway cows, mend fences, prop up leaning chimneys in windstorms, frame walls, and, with immense trepidation, how to kill small animals who were suffering from the various injuries that they incur on farms.

One day, I heard what sounded like a knock on the back door, and as I opened it, two full grown hogs came running in, shoving their way past me as I stood there shocked. They tore through the house, grunting and squealing and munching bites of houseplants on their way by, with me in furious pursuit.

The children loved life on the farm, but it had its challenging moments. I recalled one traumatic and amusing incident:

It was a sultry summer evening. Having ceremoniously tucked all four children into bed, I rejoined Bob where he was digging a new garden patch in our sixty-acre yard. There was always so much work to do. Glancing back, I noticed how the huge old Victorian farmhouse loomed against the evening sky.

We worked quietly for fifteen or twenty minutes. Suddenly, the children began shrieking wildly. Looking up, we could see them running back and forth repeatedly past the open windows.

"They'd better settle down soon or I'll have to go up there," Bob growled.

"They will, Dear. They just have a hard time relaxing when it's still light out."

The whoops and screams continued, and suddenly Leigh's curly blond head popped out the window. "Mommy, Daddy, come here right now!"

"I'll go, Dear. You go ahead and dig," I said.

I tramped back to the house and up the stairs, resenting the intrusion. With four little ones, I looked forward to my peaceful evenings a lot. When I entered the first bedroom, they all stopped running and jumped, giggling, back into their beds. "What is going on here?" I grumbled. "I thought you guys were settled for the night."

"There was a funny bird in here, Mommy." Leigh's eyes were big and round. As the oldest, he was automatically protector and spokesman. "It was black, and it didn't have any feathers, and it had ears, and it kept flapping at us." He gulped.

My stomach gave a distinct lurch, but my face remained calm and motherly. I smiled and tried to look reassuring. "That," I said calmly, "was a bat. And you're right, Leigh, it's just like a little bird. It's like a sweet little mouse with wings. It won't hurt you. It's totally harmless."

I tried to keep my eyes, which wanted to dart frantically around the room, focused on their cherubic little faces.

I noticed with relief that they all sighed, then smiled and snuggled back down into bed.

"Now I'll sing you a little song," I said in my most soothing voice.

There were more bats upstairs on subsequent evenings but fortunately always after the children were asleep. Bob became very skilled at killing them with a tennis racket, while I pulled the covers tightly over my head, shuddering.

One night, Bob had taken Weeble, our black lab puppy, to the vet. Our big Morgan mare, Jet, had stepped on him, and we feared he might have a broken leg. At bedtime, I rounded up the children and herded them up the narrow, winding front stairway. I told them I would wake them with news of Weeble when Dad got home.

As I reached the top stair, a bat suddenly swooped down, making several passes at me and flapping frantically. I screamed hysterically, swatting at it repeatedly, screeching, gyrating, and wild-eyed. Finally, the poor little thing flitted on into the upstairs blackness. I turned to see my four babes, huddled together and staring at me in sheer bewilderment and terror.

Leigh recovered quickly, giggling and pointing his chubby little finger at me accusingly. "But Mommy, you said . . . "

"Never mind," I interrupted, patting my hair and regaining my parently composure. "Let's go down and stay in the den until your father returns. We'll have popcorn."

It was years later on a visit to Carlsbad Caverns that I learned the truth about the harmlessness of most bats.

There were many good times on the farm. None of us anticipated the dark, destructive storm that was gathering. Bob and I really began to grow apart during this time. We both loved our children deeply and we did a lot of projects together—like remodeling the old farmhouse and the barn, and caring for the animals—but we were totally unable to communicate our true thoughts or feelings, including love, to each other.

We functioned in two very separate worlds. I could not enjoy sex with Bob. I was still hampered by fantasies and expectations of what a man should be, unable to love Bob for who he really was. With no counseling or outlet for our frustrations, we both sank deeper and deeper into confused, painful denial. And we never talked about any of it.

Eventually, Bob began spending more and more nights away from home, calling with various excuses. This was an acceleration of a pattern that had always been there, but I continued to pretend it wasn't that serious. I knew he was drinking heavily, was an alcoholic, but I had no idea how to help him or myself. We spiraled out of control, out of touch, out of hope.

∞

50

I was startled to notice that I was crying. I could not remember ever crying about the decline of my marriage before. More awakening feelings? I cried for quite a while, then got up from my hospital bed and went in for a shower. I felt better, more relaxed after that. I continued to see that the real value of this review of my life was not figuring everything out but unlocking some powerful storehouse of emotions I had inside, then turning it all over to my God consciousness. It felt very good. I felt like I was caring for and loving myself.

I got up and went into the bathroom to comb my wet hair. Looking in the mirror, I realized that my face looked softer, more peaceful than it had in days in spite of some lingering redness around my eyes from crying. Returning to the bed, I picked up my *Course in Miracles*. My latest habit was to just think of a concern or question, then let it fall open to a page. Why, I wondered, had Bob and I not known how to be close? What did I need to know to have a loving, intimate relationship in my life? I read:

For communication must be unlimited in order to have meaning, and deprived of meaning, it will not satisfy you completely. Yet it remains the only means by which you can establish real relationships, which have no limits, having been established by God.

(15.IX.2:5–6)

# SIX

# BETRAYED

*The betrayal of the Son of God lies only in illusions, and all his "sins" are but his own imagining. His reality is forever sinless. He need not be forgiven but awakened.*

—A COURSE IN MIRACLES (17.I.1:1–3)

Saturday, April 15, 1989—Afternoon: Loud, piercing shrieks interrupted my peaceful reverie as I lay on my bed later that afternoon. I put aside my *Course in Miracles*, got out of bed, and stuck my head out the door. I stared, transfixed by the scene taking place near the end of the hall, just inside the locked double doors. I could see three attendants and a nurse bent over the figure of a woman who was curled up in a ball on the floor, huddling against the wall.

I felt old terror as I crept out into the hall to get a better look. Between the bodies of the staff members, I could see that the woman was very old, tiny, and withered, but she was far from weak or frail. When one of the staff spoke to her, or worse, attempted to touch her, she struck at them, kicking and flailing and screaming obscenities. "Leave me the hell alone, you mother fuckers! You're not locking me up in this place again!" she wailed. In between tirades, she moaned and sobbed.

The attendants pleaded with her to no avail. Finally, glancing at me and some of the other patients who had also come out into the hall to see what the ruckus was about, two of them grabbed her by the arms and half carried, half dragged her into a room and shut the door.

It took a while for peace to be restored on the ward. I went back into my room and sat on my bed, hugging my knees to my chest. I knew what that old woman had been feeling. I was becoming convinced that no matter how crazy we seem to be, we always know on some level what is happening to us. I was learning that every human being is terrified of losing her mind, of leaving reality. Being labeled insane means you will never be quite the same again. It is a life sentence, like being a thief. Even if you are cured, who knows when you might flip out again. I realized that most of us would rather be dead than insane.

I could see how we reach out for help in whatever way we can when we know our reality is becoming distorted. And when the reaching out looks a certain way, and we are locked up, we cannot perceive this as help—and we feel ultimately, profoundly betrayed. I took a deep breath, realizing that I was becoming anxious and beginning to project my own fears and feelings into the dilemma of the poor old woman. I lay back on my bed, trying to relax.

I could not get the idea of betrayal out of my thoughts. Suddenly, I realized that I had experienced devastating betrayal before in my life, long before being unwillingly admitted to the psych ward. Obviously, I had unfinished business with this issue.

I knew I needed to bring to mind the end of my marriage with Bob. This was the next key event in my declining emotional/spiritual life that needed to be illuminated by the loving Light. Somewhat reluctantly, I closed my eyes and recalled the past, returning to the farm:

∞

I thought that I might be able to stay in my marriage if I could just find some occupation for myself. When all four of my children were finally in school for the first time, I felt an intoxicating freedom. I immediately began dreaming of doing something creative and challenging away from home. I suddenly realized how envious I had been of Bob's career.

Bob was not supportive or empathetic. He thought I had plenty to do to keep house, iron his shirts, prepare meals, be there for the kids when they came home, tend the animals and continue to remodel the house. I guess he was right in a way. What he didn't understand was my need for an autonomous existence aside from the family.

Before long, I had found a way to create this for myself. I was exhilarated to rekindle my independent nature, but Bob found this profoundly threatening.

I remembered the day my adventure began. It was early spring of 1977, and Bob and I were painting together on the huge Victorian farmhouse we had bought two years before. We had sixty acres of land, a big barn, and, like Noah's ark, two of every animal we could find. It was paradise to our four children. Though we loved it, the immense financial and energy outlay it required put a terrible strain on our already struggling marriage.

55

Bob put down his paintbrush for a moment and turned to me. "I've invited some people over on Sunday. Ben and Paula DuBarry. I work with Ben. Remember, I told you about them?"

I looked up. "Yeah, I think so."

"How's Sunday around three?"

"Sure, as long as they don't mind working on the house or watching us."

"I told them."

Old friends were used to coming out and pitching in or grabbing a beer and sitting in the yard while we hammered and painted; new ones had to be initiated. We rarely stopped to visit or relax.

On Sunday, Paula and Ben arrived as planned. I was drawn to Paula instantly, which was very unusual for me.

She was about my height with a trim figure. Her eyes and hair were brown. She had a wonderful, warm, infectious laugh. Fun just seemed to want to burst out all over her.

We all had a few beers and some hors d'oeuvres. Paula and I decided to go into the little town nearby to shop in the numerous antique stores that were its main attraction. We wandered along the charming side streets, chatting compatibly.

"I've been thinking about starting a business," Paula said, glancing around at the quaint old storefronts.

"Yeah, my kids are all in school now, and I'd like to do something too," I echoed.

She put a hand on my arm. "Maybe we should go into business together."

We both laughed. We were finding we did a lot of that. "What kind of business would we do?" I asked, still chuckling.

"Well," she said, "a friend of mine started a used clothing shop back east. It's gotten real popular there. They call them resale shops or something. People bring nice stuff they don't wear anymore and put it on consignment. When you sell it, you split the money."

"That sounds like great fun. We could fix up one of these old buildings." I too began looking around, half-serious now.

Our husbands just smiled when we went home and gushed our ideas to them. Little did they know we would be spending ten thousand dollars in the next few weeks on our little dream.

The next week, we met with Mrs. Cannon. The Cannons owned most of the finer old buildings in town, and they operated a prosperous antique business in one of the largest ones. After showing us several spaces, Mrs. Cannon took us through the basement of one old building because it was a quick way to get to the next space upstairs. The basement had been used only for storage for probably a hundred years. It was filled with piles of dirt and garbage. A rat ran in front of us, causing us all to squeal and jump. I put a hand on Mrs. Cannon's arm, stopping her in the middle of the rubble.

"How much would it be to rent this basement?" I asked.

Paula stared at me dumbfounded. Mrs. Cannon, a cool businesswoman, just raised an eyebrow and said, "Well, I don't know if you could do much with this. You could have the whole place for seventy-five a month." Her tone of voice said plainly that she thought it was impossible, that we were a couple of naive idiots.

I looked her straight in the eye. "OK. We'll talk about it and let you know."

Later, we sat in the car across the street and talked. Paula expressed her concern. "Are you nuts, Sue?"

My mind was already in design mode. "Listen, you've seen our farmhouse. I know we can make that place really great. Are you willing to try?"

Then and there, I established myself as the creative force of our team. Paula was rarely able to visualize the colorful and ambitious ideas I excitedly described to her, but she was trusting and enthusiastic and a damned hard worker. We signed a lease, informed our still smirking husbands, put on our coveralls and work boots, tied up our hair, and went at it.

It took us three days just to clean out the garbage. The whole space was over five thousand square feet. It was dark and filthy but dry. We called it Mushroom Square. We built walls. We laid brick floors. We carpeted. We cleaned out an old brick coal chute and hung a fern in it. We cleared a charming old wood freight elevator and made it the entrance to our "Fun and Funky" section, where we later featured vintage clothing.

We worked from early morning until late at night. We ached from working, and we ached even more from laughing.

We sat down at the end of the day for a beer and a cigarette and shared our deepest thoughts and feelings. We became dearest, closest friends.

We made clothes racks with chains and closet poles and hung them from solid old beams. We installed soft spotlights everywhere. We built a dressing room and a clothes storage room for sorting the consignment items. We painted some walls a fresh spring green and paneled others with genuine barn wood from our barn.

One afternoon, after nearly everything was complete, I stopped working and looked at Paula. "We need a counter," I said. "Maybe someone could make us one. We need something neat, with recessed panels and stuff—something old-fashioned. It'll be expensive." Paula just grunted. We had already spent a lot of money.

An hour later, I was tackling yet another dark corner in the unused part of the basement. We still needed more storage space and were clearing out-of-the-way spaces we had formerly passed by. Suddenly, there it was—a beautifully paneled wooden counter, exactly the size and height we needed. It was covered with about an inch of dust but otherwise was perfect. I called Paula over and we both stared in disbelief.

This was the first of many times that we needed something, only to have it appear like some magic miracle. It was during this project that I first became aware that these miraculous coincidences occur all the time in my life, especially when I am acting out of love for myself or others.

Paula and I worked in perfect unison. We were a model team, giving and taking in loving tandem. Our friendship deepened as our business relationship developed. And so, after three months of grueling, passionate labor, we were ready to open for business. Our husbands were flabbergasted but proud. Bob had given me constant flack about being away from home and the kids, but I felt it was my time and just did it.

I had designed oversized business cards describing our new business and we had them printed in blue ink on beige card stock. We placed them on the counters of businesses all over the three towns in the area. "Cash for Your Clothing," they promised.

We had no idea if anyone would show up the day we scheduled to begin taking in clothes. We were very apprehensive. What if it didn't work? What if all this had been for nothing? We were at the shop very early on the designated day. At 10 A.M., the hour we had advertised, we went up to open the door. There was a line of women, their arms loaded with clothing, clear down the block.

We were a hit. The local paper did a story on us. People even came from the nearby cities just to see our charming little underground shop—then sent their friends. We began offering plants and artwork (mine) for sale. The Cannons came down to see what all the hubbub was about. "People keep calling us looking for your store," they chuckled. They loved what we had done and congratulated us profusely.

We were making a huge percentage of profit. We immediately began grossing over two thousand dollars a month, and our overhead was just seventy-five dollars a month rent plus about twenty-five dollars in utilities. Everyone was very happy.

Paula and I became total confidantes. I don't recall exactly when the bizarre conversations began, but I remember a particular occurrence one evening after closing shop. We had turned up the stereo and were drinking our favorite red wine. We had acquired an old mannequin and loved to dress her in hilariously wild, seductive outfits and put a cigarette in her mouth. I remember that Paula was quite somber on this evening and wouldn't laugh no matter what I did to the mannequin.

"Ben is getting really weird lately," she said in a serious tone, out of the blue.

"Like how?" I stopped and looked at her thoughtfully.

"Well, he keeps imagining things. He says dumb stuff that isn't true." She seemed genuinely disturbed.

"Hmm," I muttered, not really understanding. "Maybe too many drugs," I ventured, knowing they smoked a fair amount of marijuana.

"I just don't know," she finished vaguely, then changed the subject.

Paula was to make several similar comments over the next couple of weeks. It really made no sense to me. She seemed concerned about the bizarre behavior she was attributing to Ben but never really wanted to pursue solutions. I just made some generally sympathetic remarks and let it all pass.

About a week later, as Bob and I were sound asleep in our bedroom, the phone rang at nearly 2 A.M. Bob got up and answered it.

"Who was that?" I asked groggily.

"It was Ben." His voice sounded strangled. I was now fully awake.

"What's wrong?" I whispered, not wanting to wake the children.

"He's coming right over." Now he sounded terrified, shaky.

"What is it?" I repeated.

"Something . . . wrong," his voice trailed.

Bob got out of bed, pulled on some clothes, and hurried downstairs. I just lay there quivering. I couldn't imagine what was wrong. I put on a robe and crept halfway down the kitchen stairs we had built. The stairway offered an open view, and I sat there looking down into the kitchen, where Bob was pacing with his hands over his face. I was petrified.

Suddenly, a car raced into the driveway and skidded to a halt. A dark figure got out and headed for the house. The back door was thrown open, then slammed shut. Paula ran through the kitchen and into the den, slamming that door as well. I just stared in disbelief as Bob, looking up at her as she whizzed through, continued pacing.

What in the hell was happening here?

Then another car pulled into the driveway. Another figure got out, more slowly, and came into the kitchen. Ben stood directly in front of Bob and said in a hideous voice, "I want Sue here."

"No," Bob whispered. I could hear desperation, pleading in his voice.

"I want her down here," Ben repeated, barely controlling the violent anger that was evident in his clenched fists and twitching facial muscles.

I got up stiffly and went down the stairs and into the kitchen near them. "I'm here, Ben," I said as calmly as I could. Paula had not come out of the den. The three of us stood there in a tense little circle in the middle of the night.

Ben looked at me, then glared at Bob for several seconds. He spoke slowly but with deadly menace, "You son of a bitch! I want Sue to be right here to hear this! I've had you followed by a detective! You have been fucking my wife!"

Bob looked at the floor and said nothing.

The world spun in front of my eyes. Rockets shot into far-off space in my head and tornadoes roared in my ears. They say the wife always knows on some level; this wife didn't.

I don't remember anything else that happened that night between Bob and the DuBarrys. I remember stumbling upstairs and crawling in bed with the kids and not being able to sleep. I woke up my four babies very early in the morning. I kissed them all and told them I had to go visit Grandma right away. They were young enough to accept this brief explanation.

I packed a few things and left immediately for Seattle—home to mother. I cried all the way, nearly breaking down when I passed the hospital where Jaqui had been born. My mother encouraged me to go back and save my marriage. "There's nothing better out there," she coached.

I returned to the farm. I successfully repressed once again my extreme pain and rage, this time directed at Bob. I remember rolling out of bed onto the floor a few times in the middle of the night, then rolling around the floor moaning. But I never cried, never screamed, never cut off his balls, which is what I really wanted to do.

And I never went back to Mushroom Square. Paula tried to run it alone for about six months, then gave up.

Bob and I tried therapy, we tried to talk, we tried to restore our old, fake life. We tried everything but God, whom we did not know. I could not forgive, could not cross the black gulf. It was the end. I had absolutely no way to heal this gigantic, festering wound. We divorced in 1978.

∞

62

I realized I was clenching and twisting the hospital bedsheet in my hands. I took some deep breaths and went out for a glass of water.

Feeling a little better, I decided to walk down the hall to get a little exercise. I was surprised to see that the door was open to the room where they had taken the little old woman. She was sitting on her bed in a hospital gown. One of the nurses was braiding her hair in a long white braid down her back. She smiled and talked with the nurse.

Seeing me, she called out, "Hello, Dearie. Come in, come in. I was just telling Nurse about my class this year. They are darlings!" She took my hand and looked up at me, searching my face. I felt like I could see her Soul in her tired old eyes. She sighed and asked, "Are you sad, Dearie? You seem sad. Don't worry. You'll be out of here soon. They never make us stay too long. It's really quite a nice place."

I later learned that the nurses adored her. She was truly an angel, they said. I also learned that she was a long-retired schoolteacher—and a schizophrenic.

What transformed her from a screaming animal into an angelic, little old lady and back again? Why did it happen, and why to her? Had she perhaps been profoundly betrayed once? Had she repressed some incredible pain and rage in her life that poisoned and twisted her mind beyond human repair? Had she ever been offered a chance to review her life, to heal, to remember God? Had she refused it?

I went back to my room to ask these questions of the only source of answers that had helped me and to pray for God to heal my wounds.

# SEVEN

# SPECIAL RELATIONSHIPS

*Every special relationship you have made has, as its fundamental purpose, the aim of occupying your mind so completely that you will not hear the call of truth.*

—*A Course in Miracles* (17.IV.3:3)

S aturday, April 15, 1989—Evening: My throat tightened when I read the message attached to my door. It said: "Your father and his wife will be coming to visit you this evening about 7:30." I always had this response when I thought of seeing my father.

I went in to dinner and tried to force spaghetti and meatballs down my still-constricted throat. Needing distraction, I studied the faces of the other patients. They seemed so placid, so resigned. Did they ever feel afraid of their fathers? I wondered. Were they capable of relating to anyone? Did they long for relationships and not know how to relate? I did not think one needed to be mentally ill to have that problem.

I returned to my room to prepare for my father's visit. He and Ethel, his second wife, arrived promptly at 7:30. I was surprised to see that he was carrying a beautiful Gund teddy bear. I was disarmed, moved by the sensitivity this gift conveyed.

Ethel sat quietly in the background, saying little, as usual. "We have been really worried about you," my father said. He actually had tears in his eyes. I had never known him to show this kind of concern for me before. I had assumed all my life that he did not feel much of anything for me. I was astounded at the miraculous possibility of my father loving me.

We talked about what was happening, and he seemed to feel better seeing that I looked and sounded quite relaxed and normal. He hugged me sincerely when he left. This one visit healed some of the years of accumulated emotional abandonment that I had felt in our relationship.

After he was gone, I prepared to go to bed for the night. I felt hopeful, reflective. I got into bed and hugged the soft bear, propping up pillows to sit against and think. If I can feel loved by my father, I thought, I can heal every pain I've ever felt in relationships with men. I realized that I had actually never learned how to have a loving, honest, intimate relationship with anyone. I tried again and again to get it right, but most of my relationships were replete with judgment and manipulation.

I found relationships with men the most difficult. I had felt intimidated and controlled by male authority figures— father, husband, bosses, teachers, landlords, doctors, lawyers—all my life. I was carrying a lifetime of deadly rage toward men in my heart. Yet, paradoxically, I longed desperately to be close to men, to love and be loved by them.

Nor had I achieved much true intimacy with women. I usually felt competitive with them on some level.

These relationship issues had obviously been pivotal for me in my developing confusion. The real problem was that I had never had a relationship with God, which would have given me the means to heal all my rage and judgment as I realized my own perfect innocence and that of others. I had heard of such a thing, but like a happy marriage, it was some miraculous dream that apparently happened to other people. Without a relationship with God, I could not truly love others, for I could not love myself.

I tried frantically to create new relationships in my life in the years after Bob and I divorced, but with my self-esteem at an all-time low, I entered a period of promiscuity that dominated my social life. Even my relationships with women were about looking for men.

I knew this was the next critical stage in the development of my life, the next area that needed healing. I closed my eyes and remembered these times of overpowering passion and pain:

∞

After Bob and I divorced, I really believed I wanted to form another committed primary relationship. Yet for some reason, over and over again I chose inappropriate partners. Looking back, I think I was terrified to trust any man again.

Once we decided to get a divorce in the summer of 1978, Bob moved out. I stayed with the children at the farm for a time, putting them back in school in September. I tried desperately to maintain some continuity for them. I was nearly crazy with pain, fear, and loneliness. That following winter was hard and cold—both weather-wise and emotionally. I hauled water in buckets from the neighbors' property for the horses and cows when our own water froze.

Spring came at last, and I began to look for diversion, a way to escape my feelings of isolation and pain. One day I saw an ad in the local paper for a cartoonist. I had never done cartooning. Nevertheless, I spent the weekend putting together a portfolio of cartoons and scheduled an interview.

To my amazement, the editor of the newspaper, after keeping me waiting for fifteen minutes in his office, came strolling in wearing white tennis shorts. He was about my age and possibly the most gorgeous man I have ever seen, before or since. Rhodes scholar and athlete, he had curly brown hair, hazel eyes, and the body of Adonis. His name was Todd.

Todd, the editor-prince, loved my work and hired me on the spot. A few days later, he personally came to the farm to interview and photograph me for an article on the new cartoonist. The interview took place in my studio, which I had built in the barn loft. I was looking good; I had regained my little round figure and was already lightly tan from being outdoors.

As Todd prepared to leave that day, he looked deep into my eyes and asked if I would like to go for coffee with him sometime. I declined, somewhat flustered, explaining that I was newly divorced with four children. I hadn't been approached by a man for years, but I remembered how to repel that kind of energy very well. I had been doing so from about the age of six when my mother first began to warn me about boys.

I just didn't think I was ready. I had never had sex with anyone but Bob. I didn't think it was very important to me, but I couldn't stop thinking about the editor. That night, I began to lose control to some mysteriously powerful, lustful longing. I could not sleep. I could hardly breathe. It was as though thirty years of repressed passion took over my body and mind.

I would have been shocked had I known that I was about to enter into a period of rampant promiscuity in an attempt to reassure the deeply wounded part of me that I was attractive and desirable. I thought the insatiable desire I felt was something that just happened to divorced people.

The next day I called Todd and told him I didn't know what was wrong with me, but I had to see him. I drove to his house that night, exhilarated beyond anything I had ever felt. As I approached his door, I prepared for the disappointment I was sure I would experience when this prince turned into a frog, but, indeed, the first of my large collection of pretend princes opened the door.

There were many, many men. At first, it seemed I just couldn't get enough attention and acknowledgment. I met men everywhere. I had black lovers, a Japanese lover, old lovers, young lovers, big lovers, small lovers, single and married lovers. I once met a young man on a bus, got off at his stop, and went to his house and had sex with him. Looking back, I realized that I had learned something from every encounter. Someone once said, "On some level, I loved everyone I ever had sex with." This was true for me.

Eventually, Bob took the boys to live with him. The girls and I moved into a house in the city, the first of many. I enrolled at a local university in the architecture program. Being back in school, a star again, helped me regain my old sense of security and importance and improved my self-esteem.

Architectural studies were very demanding. With less time to shop for men, I settled into a pattern of serial monogamy. However, being a college student again for the first time in twenty years also propelled me into a sort of second childhood—the wild one I never had. I partied, drinking quite a bit, dancing until dawn, and occasionally even smoking marijuana. I was drawn to extremely tempestuous, passionate people, with whom I acted out years of my own repressed passion—both positive and negative.

I remembered three of these people with whom I had formed powerful, almost obsessive relationships. I met my volatile match in my architecture professor, Craig Lambert. He brought out all my rage at male authority figures, and I challenged him regularly. I fell in love with a young Italian student named Darren Bianca and focused on sex to avoid the truth—that real, lasting intimacy with him was unlikely. And I befriended Patty Farris, an impetuous, powerful woman who intimidated and manipulated everyone, including me, but whose bewitching powers were irresistible.

These three relationships happened within a very short period of time—a climactic time of confusion and quandary for me:

69

May 1979: I stood on the brick porch of a sweeping Tudor mansion in an affluent old neighborhood; Darren's roommate was a successful architect. Nice, I thought.

I suppose all architecture students analyze every building they encounter. This was a lovely, symmetrical old house. Built around the turn of the century, it was made of stucco and half timbered with rich brown beams. The leaded windows sparkled in the morning light. Ivy climbed the posts to the porch roof and red geraniums lined a brick walk that curved and disappeared around the end of the house.

I felt an ecstatic thrill of anticipation. Darren and I had spent some time together in amiable play. We had hiked in a local park, gone to a movie, and necked in the car in front of his house for hours. He had invited me to his room on this Saturday morning to see his space.

I spent the weekend in his space—seeing it and all of Darren. There was a lot to see; he was six foot five, two hundred pounds of gorgeous Italian. He had black curly hair, sepia eyes, and a warm grin.

I had met Darren in architecture design class. I, following a life pattern of dutiful overachievement, was a superstar pupil. Darren, on the other hand, was struggling, enduring Professor Craig Lambert's scathing, heartless tongue lashings. "Whoever did this piece of garbage needs to give up the study of architecture and become a garbage collector!" Lambert would scream.

"I think you are being cruel, Craig," I would challenge him, infuriated. "People do have feelings about their work." Professor Lambert was five years my junior and not much taller than I. He was built like a truck, though, and was about as sensitive as one. We locked horns frequently, I being the somewhat motherly champion of the entire classes' feeling side.

Glaring at me, he puffed out his chest and retorted with one of his Harvard stories: "When I was a student of architecture at Harvard, we once worked for weeks on some very big, elaborate projects. The day we were done with them, my professor had us take them out to a field and put them in a circle, close together. Then he took a match and lit them." He sighed, then quoted his hallowed professor, "Never make the mistake of becoming emotionally involved with your work!"

"Bullshit, Craig," I spewed. "That's just macho male bullshit!"

We never quite saw eye to eye, but we had deep mutual respect for one another and our abilities. He gave me straight A's of course. We spent two years together at the university. Then Craig Lambert decided to start a private school of architecture. Four other students and I were to be his first graduating class and we helped him create and build the school. Ultimately, I became worn out from our battles and one day I stormed out of the school for good. Three years after that, his own board of directors fired him.

71

I knew that Darren and the others appreciated my spirit, and it was partly that which created the bond that he and I expanded into a full-blown love affair. We enjoyed each other's company very much, but there was no denying that the driving force of our relationship was pure, unadulterated lust. We had a passion that was never equaled in my life, before or since. It was what I needed to cover up my desperate longing for love.

A year or so later when we were living together (though Darren never gave up his own apartment), his mother came to visit from Texas. It was a hot summer evening. I dressed in a cool sundress and did my hair and makeup with extra care. I arrived at Darren's apartment with some apprehension. I was totally unprepared for the melodramatic, nightmarish scene that ensued.

Darren's mother was openly hostile to me. She was a large woman with jet-black hair and a red slash of a mouth. "Darren, Darling," she cooed, "whatever happened to that sweet young thing you were dating back home?"

When Darren walked by her, she pinched his ass and giggled, making some off-color remark. I couldn't even speak. I had never seen anyone behave like this. I had suspected that she and Darren had some problematic emotional tie because she frequently called him as early as 6 or 7 A.M. when we were together, and he couldn't seem to find the strength to ask her to stop it. However, I was certainly not prepared for this hysterical, vindictive behavior.

Finally, I said I had to go. Darren announced he was going with me. His mother began shrieking and gesturing wildly: "If you don't get rid of that woman, I am going to kill her!" she screamed.

72

I have never had anyone threaten my life before or since. It's a horrible feeling. Even though I knew it was an idle threat, I felt a cold chill of terror. I could see how crimes of passion occurred. I simply stared at this poor distraught creature, a woman really not too much older than I. At the time, I was thirty-five; Darren was twenty-two.

Bound in a web of sexual desire, we stayed together for another year. Then we began to realize that our age difference was a gulf we could not bridge in other areas besides sex. Tearfully, we agreed to part, taking another year to complete the parting.

Patty Farris came into my life during my relationship with Darren. I met Patty at a dinner party she gave with her then-boyfriend, Mike, who was an engineer and a friend of Darren's. At that time she lived in a magnificent penthouse apartment downtown. She sometimes gaily described herself as alcoholic and borderline manic-depressive. She was wildly promiscuous, often asserting, "I've done every man in town, and the easy ones twice."

Patty had grown up in a small town that was owned by her wealthy family. I was fascinated by her exotic tastes and hypnotized by her magnetic energy. She was extravagantly generous, but I always had the nagging feeling that I owed her something, which she might collect on her terms at any time—sort of like The Godfather.

Patty was a natural blonde and had blue eyes, but she was not so much classically beautiful as she was just wildly attractive in some mysterious way. She was hilariously funny, quick witted, and glib. She could be sincerely sensitive, thoughtful, and nurturing and could make you feel as though you were the best thing in her life.

When we went "trolling" (looking for men in bars—always classy bars), she would check the parking lots for Mercedes and Porsches before going in. "It's just as easy to fall in love with a rich man as a poor one, Susie," she coached me over and over. She often felt guilty about her behavior and would be depressed for a time. I did my best to emulate her. Together, we found temporary release from our own pain and fear in the arms of man after man.

At times I adored Patty. She had an angelic sweetness, a paradoxical innocence that was irresistibly lovable. She was a genius in the business world. She had started a pediatric home health care business some time before I met her. Her little girl, Liza, a Shirley Temple look-alike, had developed serious illnesses as an infant. Patty yearned to create a way for children to be able to be sick at home instead of alone in a hospital. The idea was brilliant and ahead of its time. Insurance carriers fought her, though, and eventually were the demise of her business.

Patty and I decided to live together. We checked the papers and found a mansion for rent. The rent was exorbitant. "Impossible," I wailed, terrified at the determined look on her face.

I knew that look. One time we had been at the local chichi pickup bar. On this night, a professional football

73

team was in town and was hanging out there. Patty was terribly nearsighted but refused to wear her glasses when we went out. She asked me to check out a man at the bar. "Susie, tell me what that guy over there looks like. I think he's the captain of the team. Is he cute?"

"Oh, Patty," I moaned, "not him. He's got seven women around him, all gorgeous. And yes, he's cute."

Patty gave me that look. She calmly picked up her purse, freshened her lipstick, fluffed her blonde hair, and moved in on the poor man. He never knew what hit him.

She read the ad for the mansion carefully. "Hmm, I think I know the man who owns this house. He's a city commissioner. If not, I'll make his acquaintance. We'll get the house," she said, Mae West-like. And we did. Patty and the commissioner had many good times in the upstairs bedroom of his mansion. We called it the Big House.

74

Patty was impulsive and wildly creative. Under her direction, we would throw impromptu Friday night dinner parties for twelve to twenty people at the Big House. She would make a series of phone calls from her satin-sheeted conference bed, then announce cheerfully, "Come on, Susie, we're doing dinner. Let's go shopping." We would then race all over town to this place and that, often spending hundreds of dollars (hers of course) on supplies and ingredients. Then she would throw together (literally) a gourmet meal worthy of a master chef. She loved to do massive pots of cioppino accompanied by numerous bottles of good red wine (she later opened a restaurant in Sun Valley). The next morning, hungover but still charming, she would dump a pile of bills out of her purse, select a few twenties, and pay the kids to clean up the kitchen, which looked as though it had been bombed.

Patty was extraordinarily seductive. She was devastating and devastated. She worshiped her father and loathed her mother: "She's been stealing my boyfriends since I was twelve."

Most of all, she was a woman of astounding contrasts. It was Patty who took me to a local church and introduced me to the beautiful Catholic ritual of Mass.

∞

I hugged the soft teddy bear my father had brought me. It was light brown with a blue ribbon tied around its neck. I felt some sadness and some guilt about my time of promiscuity and passion-based relationships. I often wondered how I could have been a very good mother during those times, but I saw clearly that I was simply doing what I had to do, the only things I knew how to do, to survive the pain.

More importantly, these were lessons that had helped me learn and grow. I was beginning to see a common element in all of my so-called negative life experiences. I was beginning to see that the purpose was for me to see the Light in them. I could see, for example, that Patty was a lot like Marla, my college friend who had been so focused on sex. Somehow these women represented my dark side, the side I had always repressed and longed to explore. The challenge for me was to understand and love these women, to embrace my own dark side, and thence to become my whole Self.

I got up from the hospital bed and went down to the nurses' station for a pill. I had hoped to sleep without medication tonight, but my father's visit, coupled with the intensity of the memories of the relationships of my architecture school days, had made me quite anxious. I had lived a much more mellow life the last four years, but I knew I was still running, still frantically searching.

I returned to my room and got into bed, settling back against the pillows. My thoughts became gradually calmer. I suddenly realized that I felt a distinct longing to simplify my life. I almost wished I could just stay here in the hospital forever. Was it possible to create this simple peace and

75

serenity in my everyday life outside? I thought it must be, and I was sure a part of it would have to be creating relationships that were more grounded, more safe, more peaceful. It would mean creating relationships that had a spiritual base.

# EIGHT

# DIVINE LIGHTNING

*The most dramatic signs of Kundalini awakening are physical and psychological manifestations called kriyas. One can experience intense sensations of energy streaming up the spine, violent shaking and spasms.*

—Dr. Stanislav Grof, Psychiatrist
Christina Grof

S unday, April 16, 1989—Afternoon: It was Easter Sunday. I felt that there was something special, something newly significant about that for me, but I did not know what it could be. There was no evidence of Easter in any of the routine activities on the psych ward. Although there was no one on the ward with whom I could share, my unexplained feelings of awe and excitement remained with me all morning as I showered and ate.

After lunch my three children, Jaqui, Erik, and Libbi, arrived to visit. They walked into my room close together, as if needing comfort and support from one another to face this fearful situation of their mother locked up in a loony bin. Libbi and Erik, in their late teens, were still deeply bonded in spite of separate living environments. They sat next to each other on the two chairs. Jaqui perched tentatively on the end of my bed like a tiny frightened bird. Her freckles were pronounced in her pale little face. She was twenty-one.

They all just stared at me for a moment, not saying anything. I knew they were upset. Ordinarily they would all have been jabbering at once, competing for my attention to hear their latest news. I did not have any timid children. I stretched out my arms to them. "Come hug me. I hate to disappoint you, but I am not going to do or say anything weird."

They all got up slowly and came and hugged me, one by one. When they realized that I was crying, they seemed surprised at first, then they visibly softened. "It's OK, Mom," Jaqui spoke for them. "We love you."

I felt loved, but I also wanted them to understand. "I'm in the wrong place, you guys. You all know how I've been having strange spiritual experiences. Well, I became totally freaked out about it. I just couldn't handle it anymore. Dr. Ryan and Grampa were both confused. They thought I was suicidal or something. That's why I was brought here." They looked brighter, interested. "But I'm not suicidal—never was—and believe it or not, this place has been perfect for me. I'm feeling almost normal again. I've been doing a lot of thinking, and I think I'm beginning to understand the whole thing." I told them all about the incidents in the hospital, how I had related them to my life, and how I was beginning to see my life differently, to see God in everything.

I looked at Jaqui. Her head was cocked sideways, her eyebrows raised slightly over her big round blue eyes. "But Mom, Grampa said he thought you were taking some drugs or something."

"No, Dear, no drugs. Only the Xanax that Dr. Ryan herself prescribed for me when this first happened. Xanax is a special medication for anxiety. However, I never saw Dr. Ryan—she just prescribed for me over the phone one time early in my illness. Dr. Doughton, who Grampa doesn't trust because he needs someone to blame, has been treating me ever since." Bob Doughton, an M.D. turned counselor, was a member of my church and an old friend. I had been seeing him during my latest episode of emotional distress. He believed I was having a spiritual experience but had not learned the skills to help me. "And he," I continued, "simply gave me more Xanax. They're giving me Xanax here at the hospital as well. It wasn't the drugs. I'm still not sure what it is, but it's not drugs."

Erik spoke. He sounded tender, sincere. "Well, I trust you, Mom. Whatever you say is good enough for me. I've just been worried sick about you. I'm so glad to see you. You seem fine to me—same as always." The relief was visible in his face. He was a handsome nineteen-year-old blonde, with the lean hard body of a jock. He still had his dimples and his loving nature.

"Yeah, Mom. You seem fine," Libbi echoed.

"I am fine, Honeys. I'm so, so glad you all came. I've been dying to see you." They all hugged me tightly as they left, telling me again how much they loved me.

As she was about to walk out the door, Jaqui suddenly turned around and reached into her purse, "I almost forgot, Mom. Your friend, Sandy, stopped by just before we left and asked me to give you this. It's a tape of the Easter service at church this morning." I felt tears spring to my eyes again. Sandy was my dearest old friend from architecture school. We had become very close, and lately we had both discovered a wonderful new church called the Living Enrichment Center (LEC). How had she known how much I had longed to attend Easter service this morning? "She said to tell you she loves you. She will be up to visit soon. She wanted to give your family time to come see you first."

"Thank you, Jaqui. Thanks a lot. I'll listen to this as soon as I can get to a tape recorder." I hugged her again.

After the children left, I lay back and thought about them, about how incredibly dear they were to me. I wondered how I would have made it through all those years if it hadn't been for my children. The growing darkness had

79

nearly overwhelmed me, I recognized as I reviewed my life, and it was largely my love for my children that had kept me in touch with God, kept me going toward the Light.

I felt deeply moved realizing that they had loved me, never doubting me or complaining, through it all—including the last four years of growth and change in me and the periods of spiritual insanity. I worried about the effects it must have had on them. Four years ago, my whole life as I knew it had come to a screeching halt as I suddenly had become overwhelmed and incapacitated with mysterious, mystical energy. This must have overturned their world as well.

I knew it was time to think about the last four years. Somehow, the visit of my children gave me the strength to face the memories of the bizarre, jarring events that were a part of this time. I closed my eyes, remembering how it all began:

∞

The Big House, 1985: Patty Farris and I had moved into the three-story, seven-bedroom mansion near a large park on the east side with her little daughter, Liza, and three of my four kids. Erik lived with his father. For several months, Patty and I and our children had acted out our little survival dramas in an elegant atmosphere of stained glass, dark hardwood paneling, and high beamed ceilings. Then Patty suddenly decided to move out on one of her wild whims. I had been devastated by her abandonment—and at being stuck with eight hundred dollar a month rent payments.

My work at that time was exciting but very challenging. I had graduated from college with honors and was doing residential remodeling design. I loved my job, but I was working on commission and that was stressful for me. I presented my usual picture of perfection—loving mom, talented designer, passionate lover—to the world, but inside where it really mattered, in the depths of my soul and my deepest secret heart, I was plunging ever more deeply into a dark morass of fear and confusion.

One ominous, powerful night I hit bottom:

It was 2 A.M. on January 12, 1985. I was in bed in my huge, second-floor bedroom at the Big House. A new lover, Michael, an architect, was in bed beside me. Michael was about ten years older than I. He was balding and had kind blue eyes, which now blinked at me uncomprehendingly. I glared angrily at him. "I just don't think we're sexually compatible. I think you'd better leave," I said evenly.

Without a word, Michael got up, dressed, and left. I reached for my journal, preparing to describe this latest little drama in my erratic love life. I noticed an entry made a few days earlier: "I'm still dating Michael, but I'm losing interest. He makes a lot of money and he's nice, but he has some kind of block about oral sex." I felt a mixture of guilt and dismay. I lay there wondering how I could be so cruel. This gave way to frustration. I just couldn't seem to find the Prince. What I hadn't learned yet was that my criteria was skewed. I thought I loved men. There had been dozens of them in my life and in my bed since my divorce, and I had thought I loved them all.

I was drawn to some other journal entries from this week in 1985. One said: "For the last week or so I've been feeling a strange pressure in my head and I have this annoying, constant cough. Sometimes I feel spacey, almost like I'm high, and I feel strange sensations when I'm driving; it's like the car is standing still and the scenery is moving. I made an appointment today with an ENT doctor." I thought I must have a low-grade sinus infection or something; perhaps that was the cause of my irritability and impatience with Michael.

Another entry stated: "I'm worried about work. I can't go back to Creative Contracting. I don't know what I'm going to do." I had recently resigned a dream job as a designer for a remodeling company called Creative Contracting. The owners, Ron and Pete, were nice guys and we had become good friends. They had risked a lot to train and support me and were hurt and angry when I told them I was leaving to accept a position with another remodeling company. The owner of this new company had flattered my ego and promised me a great deal more money. One month later, just two days before this night with Michael, she had filed bankruptcy, and I had found myself unemployed. This, too, was contributing to my short temper.

I sat up and lit a cigarette, feeling pretty purposeless, but no more than during any other lull in my life—or so I thought. I got up to go to the bathroom. The hallway was long and about seven feet wide on the second floor of the big old mansion.

As I sat there in the quiet bathroom, thoughts of Patty's abandonment and of all my other present predicaments triggered feelings of fear, fury, and deep pain, which I repressed as usual. Sitting in the dark on the toilet, I was aware only of feeling vulnerable and tense and terribly, terribly alone.

Suddenly, a powerful electrical impulse began at my tailbone and traveled up my spine to my head. It felt like my brain was exploding and frying. I couldn't move. As it abated gradually, I rose and walked shakily back to bed. I lay there with profound fear firmly grasping my mind like a vise grip. What could have caused such a sensation—a brain tumor? Was it some kind of seizure?

As the fear thoughts increased, I was suddenly gripped by violent tremors in both legs, and the electrical impulses began coursing again—this time through my entire body, clear out to my fingertips. They were much more intense than the initial attack and lasted for several minutes.

Thoroughly terrified now, I got up and crossed the bedroom, stiff legged, to the phone. Upon dialing my mother's number in Seattle, I heard her voice, sleepy but strong as usual.

"Mom, something is really wrong with me," I whispered frantically.

"What is it, Susie?"

I told her what was happening: "It seems physical," I said, "but I also feel as if my mind is splitting in two, and I'm having trouble concentrating on the present. I keep thinking very weird thoughts."

My mother had recently graduated from college with a degree in psychology. "Sounds like you are having a really bad time," she said. "Do you think you can hold on until tomorrow? I'd like to sleep a couple more hours, then head down if you think you can make it till then. It sounds like a stress reaction, anxiety, nerves."

"OK, Mom," I whispered. "I think I feel better already. I'll see you tomorrow."

"Do you think you can go to sleep now?" she asked.

"I'll try. I think I can," I responded, feeling more relaxed.

I walked, still stiffly, back to the bathroom and ran a tub full of hot water. I felt strangely light, detached from reality. I took a long, steamy bath, but my mind continued to race. I went back to bed. I could not sleep. I could not understand what was happening to me. I was quite sure at times that I was losing my mind. At other times, I was convinced that I had a brain tumor that had burst.

Time seemed to lose meaning. I shook and sizzled with electric shocks. Then my thoughts would become jumbled and meaningless, and I had the distinct feeling that my mind was literally splitting in two. I believed it might be the onset of schizophrenia.

I was surprised when I looked at the clock to find that it was already 10:30 A.M. Suddenly, I was seized with a particularly vicious physical attack. My head felt like it was literally going to burst, and my body was paralyzed and jangled with the electrical sensations I had already come to dread.

I crept down the stairs to find Libbi fixing her breakfast. She stared at me. I could see my fear reflected in the dark blue pools of her eyes. "Mom, what's wrong!" she gasped.

"I don't know, but I think I'm dying," I whispered. "Call an ambulance."

"Mom, go lie down!" she said, heading for the phone. She dialed 911 and ordered the ambulance.

When she responded to my urgent request, I noticed that I felt oddly comforted and loved. It seemed totally foreign to me, almost spiritual, as if she were some kind of angel or holy being.

I stood dumbly, waiting for her to finish, then took the phone and called my good friend, Alan Jones. I had met Alan in design class in architecture school. Not romantically attracted, we had become instant, intimate buddies. He was one of the warmest, most sensitive men I had ever known. "Alan, something is terribly wrong with me. I think I'm dying," I said. My voice was a hoarse whisper.

He laughed nervously. "What are you talking about? What's wrong? Are you serious?"

"I don't know," I told him. "Something very extraordinary, very frightening, very . . . " I trailed off.

"I'll come over as soon as I can," he said. I could hear the loving concern in his voice, and again I felt a warm sensation.

At that moment, the big ornate front door swung open, and my mother swept in with a "take charge" assurance in her step.

"We called an ambulance," Libbi said.

"Well, cancel it," said my mother. "I'll take care of things now. Everything will be fine."

Libbi looked confused and frightened.

"It's OK," my mother reassured her granddaughter. "She's just been under a lot of stress. She'll be fine."

My mother was then sixty-one. She was about five foot six. She wore her hair, now brown and white, short and permed. Her eyes had faded to a softer blue. She was outspoken and articulate, bright and self-reliant. She had divorced my father when I was twenty, and shortly thereafter, in her early forties, she had toured Europe entirely by herself.

She then returned to New Jersey where she lived with my younger sisters, Linda and Lisa, and my brother, Keith. A year later, she married the next-door neighbor, a recent widower with two small boys of his own. This lasted for six years. Then, resolutely alone for good, she set about finding herself. She did some therapy and read early self-help books, eventually becoming involved with Ken Keyes Jr. and his Living Love movement.

At the age of fifty-five, she enrolled in college for the first time and studied humanistic psychology. She graduated with high honors at the age of fifty-nine. Feeling that she had truly become a totally different person from the naive young girl who had married my father, she changed her name from Mary Ellen Hayley Sanders to Suli Marsh.

She was here at the Big House—and I was glad to see her.

I realized how supportive the quiet atmosphere here at the hospital was for processing my memories of these powerful experiences. I was relieved to notice that I could think about the onset of the tremors and the terrors of that first horrific night in 1985 without triggering them again now. I was healing.

Inspired by the loving support of my children, I was strengthening my belief that the love of God, in the form of the Holy Spirit, had been the powerful energy that had

85

possessed my body and mind that night. Having no context for recognizing it, I had been overwhelmed by it.

I was later to learn that in the culture and spirituality of India, this force is called the Kundalini and that an experience identical to mine is known as Kundalini awakening. Moreover, as a spiritually transforming experience, it is welcomed and sought after. Nonetheless, its power can be overwhelming without knowledgeable guidance and support.

# NINE

# MIND WARS

*Many spiritual emergencies have episodes that are distinctly spiritual or "transpersonal" in content. We can actually feel that we have become things that we ordinarily perceive as objects outside of ourselves, such as other people, animals, or trees.*

— DR. STANISLAV GROF, PSYCHIATRIST
CHRISTINA GROF

Sunday, April 16, 1989—Late afternoon: The intense energy of this Easter Sunday continued as my mother came to visit around four o'clock. I sat up quickly when she entered my hospital room. I always felt a little guilty and afraid when encountering my mother. I knew these were very old feelings associated with her.

"Hello, Dear," she said. I thought her voice sounded a little too cheerful, like she was worried but not wanting to show it. "How are you?" She did not touch me but pulled up the chair and settled on it, looking at me intently.

"I'm OK now, Mom." I told her all about what had happened, how her daughter had come to be locked up on a mental ward. I told her that I felt it was all a mistake, but one which was proving rather interesting and healing.

She approved of my positive attitude, asking a number of questions: How long would I be there? Was there anything I needed? Had I seen the children? She told me she would talk to them, help them to understand. I could sense her underlying love, though as usual, she did not express it directly.

Somehow, no matter how it was expressed, I realized that I could use her love to heal. I also intuitively felt that deep in her Soul she longed to believe in the spiritual nature of my experience. I was relieved that she did not discount it. Though she had done a lot of personal growth work, she continued to exclude direct spiritual expression and practice from her life. I shared more from my heart after that insight, and we talked for over an hour.

After my mother left, I lay down on my bed and thought about her for a long while. She had come all the way from California. She always came when I cried out for help. We still had a lot of work to do to create a truly intimate, honest, and affectionate relationship, but as she had gained understanding about herself and her own painful childhood, she became increasingly supportive in my life.

I remembered the last time she had come when I cried out to her in similar distress—that morning in January 1985 at the Big House. Playing the dual role of mother and counselor, she had helped as the terrifying and electrifying sensations of the previous night continued in a series of events that I today refer to as the First Episode:

∞

My mother had taken charge of things at the Big House. She settled me on the couch with a blanket and organized the household, telling everyone to go on as usual, that I just needed some peace and quiet and rest. "So tell me what you're feeling now," she asked, focusing her attention on me.

"It's so scary, Mom. It comes and goes. I have these horrible electrical shock waves over and over again all through my body. My mind feels split, like it must feel to be schizophrenic or something. It's like there's a tug of war between good and evil. I know that sounds so bizarre. It's hard to explain. Then there've been other extraordinary things happening to me lately. I've been having these odd sensations when I'm driving." I told her about the feelings about the landscape moving while the car stood still.

My mother looked thoughtful. "Hmm. Sounds like you've been having quite a time," she responded. "Was there anything else?"

"Yes," I said. "A few weeks ago I took Liza, Patty's little girl, to the zoo. I was looking at this exhibit of penguin skeletons in a glass box. I suddenly noticed how similar they were to the human skeleton we studied in life drawing class. Then I had a sudden thought that felt like lightning struck my brain. It was simply a realization that I am an animal exactly like the penguin. It seemed so basic, so profound. I felt like I was looking down on the Earth and seeing all humans as just a big herd of animals roaming around. I looked back at the penguin and suddenly felt that I wasn't just *like* the penguin—I *was* the penguin—as though I was one with the penguin. These were all just thoughts, but I felt shaky, sort of awed and scared. It was like they were coming from a different place in my mind—some place I'd never accessed before."

My mother looked patient and interested.

"What do you think that means?" I asked her somewhat frantically.

"I don't know," she said frankly, "but it doesn't sound that bad. I wouldn't say it means there is anything seriously wrong with you."

She maintained this cool, calm logic about everything that happened for the next three days. I knew she was not feeling totally confident, however. Within hours of her arriving, I noticed that she had done something that revealed some deep concern about my mental state; she had removed an article about Jane Stanley's suicide that I had attached to the refrigerator. Jane had died a few years

89

before, but my friend, Charmien, had just sent me the article in a letter.

I pointed out to her that it had come to my attention. "I'm not depressed," I told her. "I don't think we have to worry about that. You know, I feel sad about Janey's death, but mostly I just can't understand how I can have been so close to her and not had a clue."

My mother nodded. "I think we often feel terribly alone in this culture—even when we are surrounded by family and friends." There was a sadness in her voice. "I've read that some doctors think loneliness is the number-one cause of illness. I think people commit suicide slowly, that it's a process rather than an isolated incident."

As a recent graduate in psychology, my mother was up on these things. She had come to me in this crisis, positive that together we could get through it. Fresh from her college courses and workshops and hours of reading about therapeutic counseling, she was sure she could help me. Yet she struggled when it came to giving me what I probably needed even more than intellectual understanding of my process; crippled by her own childhood wounds, she was still unable to hold me, to touch me, to be overtly tender and sweetly caring. She had pretty much eliminated these practices in my early adolescence, probably about the time she herself was abandoned by her dying mother to her abusive father.

My mother did give me a lot of wonderful support, however. I was terrified and determined to stop whatever was happening to me, seeing it as primarily destructive. She intuitively knew that I needed to go through it. Despite her agnosticism, her own troubled Soul recognized the struggles of a fellow Soul to come to the Light. From that deep wellspring that is the love we truly are, she continued to contribute powerfully to my transformation.

Time after time, hour after long hour, she patiently acknowledged, then tried to allay my fears:

"Mom, I think I'm having a nervous breakdown."

"I understand, Dear, but there's no such thing. The nerves can't break down."

"Mom, I think I'm losing my mind. It's like a literal thing, Mom. It's like the Devil or something is trying to get my mind over to a dark side. I can feel this actual struggle, like my mind has two parts and the good side keeps trying to save me but the black is so big and so powerful, it just keeps seeming like it's going to win and I'm going to lose my mind to it."

"I hear you, but you can't lose your mind, Dear. You're strong. Just try to relax. There is something for you to learn from this. Remember the Living Love reprogramming phrases? Let's try one again."

I would obediently do some of this rational emotive type therapy. Sometimes it would clear my mind for a time, and I would feel better. Then it would all start again. "It's like I want to go to the Light side, Mom. It's like I have to stay awake and stay vigilant though. If I go to sleep, I know the Dark will get me."

"It's OK. It can't get you. It just feels that way. Don't try to stop it; just go with it."

We spent many hours in the den on the first floor. My mother brought pads and blankets, and we sat or laid down on them. When she could no longer stay awake, she would doze off for brief periods, but she would always come back to alertness if it got really bad for me. I remained elated, excited, anxious, wired. There was no letup, no possibility of sleep. And it seemed as though the longer I went without sleep, the more terrified I became that the insomnia itself was an indication that something catastrophic was happening to my mind.

I knew I had to let my mother get some sleep. "You go ahead and sleep, Mom," I told her, but my fear would increase the moment she closed her eyes because then I felt alone, abandoned.

Sometimes the terror would suddenly abate and I would experience a period of quiet serenity. At these times, just as I had previously felt a strong presence of what seemed to be evil power trying to capture my mind, I now felt some sense of a glorious Good, equally potent. I had insights about all sorts of global crises and the foibles of humankind. I felt benevolent and wise, almost goddesslike, but I was never able to maintain these states.

I called a psychiatrist from the phone book. He was patient, and he responded to everything I said, but he seemed cool and uncaring to me somehow. At times I would become extremely frustrated at how calm everyone seemed. It was as though they were patronizing me. Obviously, something was very seriously wrong with me, I thought. I could never understand how come people didn't get excited and upset about the astounding, devastating thing that was happening to me.

Late on the second day of panic and trauma, I insisted that my mother take me up to a nearby hospital emergency room, which she did. There was only a young intern available from the psych department. I was able to communicate from a part of my reality that I called my Rational Observer when describing my experiences to doctors and others. I would describe the turmoil and horror I was feeling in a calm, detached manner. The student doctor was patient and mildly curious but offered no diagnosis, no treatment. My mother, terrified of drugs, insisted that I did not need and should not take any medication. So the student nodded and grunted a few times, then sent us home, telling us to call back if things got a lot worse.

Much of what was happening to me was obviously perplexing to my mother, though she never discounted it. I kept describing feelings of intense pressure, " . . . sort of in my sexual organs, but not really sexual . . . sort of farther back, hard to explain." She frowned slightly, offering no explanation for this, though later she told me she had wondered if this might have been related to something called chakras—energy centers that opened during something called a Kundalini awakening, a spiritual phenomenon that she had read about somewhere but knew little about.

On the morning of the third day, I went to see a therapist who led a women's support group I attended at Lutheran Family Services. She seemed as detached and unaffected as the others. To some extent, I was wearing a mask with the doctors and counselors, repressing my feelings, doing my "I am as intelligent and able to cope as you" act. I had a terrible fear of being affirmed as crazy as I sometimes felt.

And so, perhaps not being able to figure out what was wrong with me, these professionals were unwilling to commit to an opinion about my condition. However, it also seemed clear to me that there was something lacking in their skills and education that they seemed so perplexed by my experience. These were educated mental health professionals. At other times I felt that they just truly did not feel any compassion for me. It felt like they were clinical, apathetic.

93

Late on the third day, I had my previously scheduled appointment with Dr. John Stark, the ear, nose, and throat doctor. I kept this appointment because my sinuses were still feeling stuffy and pressured, and I coughed continually. Later I learned that these were just more of my symptoms of anxiety.

I had not slept for seventy-two hours.

Dr. Stark asked my mother to wait in the waiting room. We sat facing each other, quite close, on two chairs in his office. As I looked at his face and into his eyes, I thought he was the kindest looking person I had ever seen. I suddenly recalled that everyone had looked like this to me when I was a small child.

His voice was warm and serene, but clearly concerned. "Please tell me what is happening for you."

Tears gushed from my eyes as I told him everything that had been happening.

Dr. Stark listened attentively, then waited patiently for my sobs to subside. His voice was soft, caring. "My God," he finally said, "I can't believe the way you've been treated. I can't believe someone hasn't helped you. You are obviously an honest, intelligent human being in incredible pain." He sighed, then continued, "I read the report from your visit to the emergency room and to the psych clinic. The intern just didn't have a clue."

His words were hypnotic to me. "It seems to me that you are experiencing an extended episode of acute anxiety or panic attacks. We are just beginning to really study this phenomenon in contemporary society as it quite suddenly seems to be increasing dramatically. We don't know why. You need to look at what's going on in your life that has you so worried, but first, you just need to sleep and regain your strength. You are exhausted and depleted."

He smiled. "I'm going to give you some medication to help you sleep. I would give you a shot, but I'm afraid you would fall down in the parking lot." He chuckled. He didn't touch me physically, but I felt enveloped in his warmth and love. Finally someone understood. Someone heard me—someone who could really help me.

From the moment I entered Dr. Stark's office and began to experience his authentic loving-kindness, the astounding energy that still reverberated through my being assumed a totally different aspect. My whole world suddenly became beatific. I had visions of everyone on Earth experiencing only love and joy and bliss. I entered into a state of ecstasy, of high euphoria.

When we arrived back home, I asked my mother to make my bed downstairs on the living room couch. I felt that I had to be near everyone. Suddenly, my family appeared unearthly to me, like translucent Light Beings. Their voices were soothing and harmonious. There was soft laughter and joy all around me as though they were ecstatic with the shift in my demeanor.

I couldn't understand where these incredible, overwhelming feelings, like warm waves of love engulfing me, were coming from. I didn't want to go to sleep. I wanted to just stay in the beautiful living room of the Big House forever, surrounded by these angels who were my mother, my children, and my friends.

Eventually, I took the prescribed medication and slept for fifteen hours. When I awoke, the heavenly state was still with me. Though I considered this time of sleep to be the end of my First Episode, the euphoria actually lasted, dissipating slowly, for days.

An aspect of this euphoric state was that I felt compelled to get closer to people, to be deeply honest with everyone. I told many people in my life exactly what had happened to me. I felt pretty silly sometimes, afraid that they would think this was odd, but they never did. They usually got kind of a wistful, faraway look in their eyes and just smiled, as though they felt some mystical, empathetic understanding of my experience.

I wrote a letter to Dr. Stark's supervisor, expressing my gratitude and admiration.

Gradually, my euphoria from this remarkable three-day episode was replaced with the same old fears and frustrations of work, kids, and relationships as before. Though I knew something had begun to shift in me, it was very elusive and not quite clear. I yearned for more of whatever it was, but I was quite certain that I did not want to go through any more horrible tremors and distressing states of madness to find it!

∞

I got up from the hospital bed and went to the window. I looked out at the freeway, feeling a strange longing to know the people inside the endless stream of speeding cars.

I realized that I was wanting to know and love all people everywhere. Could that be the "something more" for which I had yearned at the end of my First Episode?

I suddenly realized that it was definitely a part of it, and that this was yet another of the valuable insights I was having here in this hospital. This time of realization had been a long time coming. After my First Episode, I had entered a four-year period of powerful spiritual growth and learning which had culminated in another Dark Night of the Soul—my Second Episode, which made my First Episode seem mild.

I noticed the beauty of the Easter sun. Filtered through the city's haze, it was a magenta orb, nearing the horizon in a peach spring sky. Suddenly, I realized that I could see the cross that had so deeply impacted me when I first arrived at the hospital. It sat atop the tower at the far end of the hos-

pital building complex. How could I not have seen it before? I wondered.

The cross was becoming a powerful sign for me. There were things about Christianity that troubled me, but I believed in the Love that Jesus taught, the understanding and forgiveness that he represented, and the promise of eternal life that was conveyed in his resurrection and celebrated on this day. The cross symbolized all these for me.

I gazed at the cross in the fading rose light and said a little prayer.

# TEN

# SAWTOOTH NIGHTMARE PLUNGE

*It is well known that the spiritual path has a variety of difficulties and pitfalls that can occasionally lead to serious psychological and even physical complications. What spiritual awakening requires of us is a willingness to face pleasure and pain equally, to open, to touch what Zorba called "the whole catastrophe."*

—Dr. Jack Kornfield, Buddhist Monk and
Psychologist

97

S unday, April 16th, 1989—Evening: My mind and body were filled with anxious thoughts and feelings later on that Easter evening. Seeing my children and my mother had been taxing and emotional. I showered and crawled into my cool bed, but I still felt tense. Though I had already taken my meds, sleep would not come. I wandered down to the nurses' station.

"What's wrong, Hon?" one of the nurses asked me.

"I can't sleep, even with my meds."

"Have you tried a sleep tape?"

"A tape? I don't have any."

"We do."

"I don't have anything to play it on."

"We do. Go on back to your room, Dear. I'll bring it right down."

A few minutes later, the nurse brought me a tiny personal tape player known as a Walkman and several soothing sleep-inducing tapes. After she left, I placed the soft foam pads of the earphones over my ears and listened to part of a tape. I couldn't believe how quickly it transported me to a place of peace. It was wonderful. I suddenly realized that I had intended to buy myself a tape player for months, but the kids always needed something more. They had stereos and all the latest fads and fashions.

I began to cry, filled with grief for my own lost Self. I saw how I had neglected my own needs with an absolute lack of loving compassion for myself. Oh, I had selfishly acquired many things that gave me status and met my ego needs, and I met my basic survival needs, but when it came to honoring my needs for peace and joy and love, I had no idea how to give these to myself.

I placed the Walkman on my nightstand and lay back against the pillows, intending to listen to a tape and go to sleep, but my thoughts continued. I remembered reading in Alice Miller's book about how high achievers often have low self-regard. I knew this was true of me, and that it was reflected in the up and down cycles of my life. I would plunge into projects, accomplishing amazing things for a while, then inevitably they would burn out—and so would I. I would feel discouraged and frustrated until the next job or relationship came along.

It occurred to me that this might be a manic-depressive cycle, and I again wondered if I was manic-depressive. I decided that I was definitely not, that my ups and downs were not that extreme, that they were a normal life pattern for someone who had no grounding force in her life. I knew I needed a spiritual focus to center my being.

I remembered how I had felt different for a while after my First Episode but had then experienced the usual surge of positive creative energy, followed by the usual failures and feelings of worthlessness. At one point, my self-esteem had become so low that I was afraid I would not be cared for if I were seriously ill or hurt.

Though I had been totally unaware of it, I had entered into a time of profound spiritual growth. For the next four years, I was to have a series of experiences and relationships that would teach me compassion, humility, and love and slowly bring me to God consciousness.

One of the first of these amazing experiences was an accident that occurred to reassure me that I did matter in the Universe and could always get care when I needed it. I remembered it well. I was struggling with another major career crisis at the time. I was also in another tumultuous relationship, and though it didn't last, this relationship was to teach me a lot about compassion for others. I closed my eyes, thinking back to this time:

For some time after my First Episode in the Big House, I tried to find out what had caused it. Most doctors and counselors felt that I had experienced severe anxiety attacks. They couldn't determine the cause themselves, but they gave me books to read. No one had much to say about the spiritual aspects of my experience. They could not explain my feeling of having overcome some powerful, dark force. I was unable to qualify for a newly formed panic and anxiety program at a local hospital because I had no medical insurance. So eventually I gave up trying to get help.

Because I couldn't afford the high rent, I moved out of the Big House shortly after my First Episode and rented an apartment. The girls lived there with me. Leigh had gone off to college, and Erik, fourteen, was still with his dad.

The euphoria that followed my First Episode eventually subsided, and I soon took up my old workaholic habits to avoid my growing spiritual unrest. I heard about a project management company called The Evergreen Group that wanted to start a remodeling operation. Approaching the owner, I convinced him to let me do it for him, and it was an immediate success.

One day a few months later, in the summer of that same year, Erik asked if I would take him fishing, then added, "Wouldn't it be neat, Mom, if there was a phone number you could call and they would tell you the best place to take a kid fishing?" I began thinking about the idea and my creative juices took over. I created a company called Telefax Inc. using Erik's idea. It was one of the first computerized, interactive telephone information systems in the country. I used Dectalks, Digital Equipment Corporation's brand new digitized-voice talking computers. I raised thirty thousand dollars in investment capital, formed a board of directors, and played for a whole year with this fun business toy.

For several months I ran both The Evergreen Group remodeling operation and the developing Telefax. Gradually, Telefax began to be too demanding, and I left The Evergreen Group—another bitter parting like the one I had experienced when I left Creative Contracting, months before. Eventually running out of money, I also disbanded Telefax.

After I had started and crashed these two major businesses, I then went back to work for Creative Contracting. Old friends and owners, Ron and Pete, had forgiven me for having left them and we were soon having as much fun as in the old days, but I felt that I was just filling time and surviving. I agonized over the instability of my work life, the seemingly endless failures and restarts.

During this period, I was embroiled in yet another fiery relationship. Ironically, this man had been introduced to me by Patty Farris, who had come back into my life for a time. I had found myself as helpless as ever to resist her charms in spite of how she had abandoned me. She had a new job as the only female lumber broker in town. "It's easy, Susie," she told me. "You just have to be hot and provocative over the phone." One evening, she invited me for drinks after work to meet one of her work buddies, Dan Hill.

Dan evoked a depth of response in me that I didn't know existed. He was another of those alive, intensely passionate people I seemed to be drawn to during this time. He brought out the full gamut of my deepest feelings—from intense love to intense hate.

We had great sex, of course. Dan was big and athletic with sandy hair and blue, blue eyes. He was expressive and loved to laugh and he adored me openly and vociferously. We also had vicious fights. Dan had uncontrollable fits of rage that were terrifying to me. He never touched me in anger, but he was ferocious as a grizzly bear. He sometimes projected blame on me for things that hurt or angered him. At my pleading, he sought counseling while we were together.

The most powerful element in this relationship for me, however, was the stimulation of another of my little-used feelings: at times I felt almost overwhelming compassion for Dan. In counseling, Dan discovered that his rage was rooted in his Vietnam experience. I would never forget the story he had told me on the first night we met. He said he had never been able to tell it to anyone, though it had happened over twenty years before. Tears flowed down his cheeks as he talked:

> In 1968, I was an Air Force medic, eighteen years old. My company was shipped to Nam. Then we were ordered into Laos.

His tone turned bitter.

> Officially, we were never there. We became trapped by the Cong. We radioed for help, but it was impossible for them to get to us. Ninety percent of my outfit— ninety percent of my buddies—were hit. Most of them were killed. I did what I could. I got pretty crazy. I ran

101

around stuffing their arms and legs into a bag and somehow made it back.

They shipped us back to Texas—the few of us who lived. We landed in the middle of the night at the far end of the runway. We got no welcome, no thank-you, no medals. They just discharged us.

I never told anyone about it—not my parents, not my wife—not even my boys.

I was deeply moved by this story and honored that Dan chose to share it with me, but in spite of our strong physical and emotional ties, we were unable to commit to one another. I found myself criticizing his unsophisticated taste in clothes and furniture, which wounded him deeply. Our relationship was unable to survive a crisis that developed one night in October 1986, when we had been together about a year. I recalled this incident:

I lay curled on my side facing Dan, huge and snoring beside me in his bed. I reached out and laid my hand on his arm. He muttered and reached around to encase it in his big warm paw. I could not sleep. I was worried and stressed. Not only was I frustrated and confused about my career, but I was beginning to question my relationship with Dan.

I had been suffering from severe insomnia for several months. I would sometimes be able to go to sleep initially at a reasonable hour, but I would wake up night after night just after midnight. My mind would race with fears and concerns. I could not stop it. Then I would become terrified that I would not get enough sleep for work the next day. This then became a self-fulfilling prophecy as I lay awake for the remainder of the night.

I had begun to self-medicate for my insomnia. On this night, I had drunk several glasses of wine and taken some sleeping pills. Eventually I was able to stop the endless chain of thoughts that excited my mind and I turned out the light, falling into a restless sleep.

Dan had just moved into an apartment from his house in the suburbs. We had often spent the night at his house, and it was my first night to stay with him here in his new place.

About 3 A.M. I got up to go to the bathroom. I was groggy and it was very dark. I took the route that I always took to Dan's bathroom—in his old house. I forgot that I was in his new apartment, and I didn't turn on the light. I walked slowly out the bedroom door with my hands extended in front of me. When I turned left and stepped through the doorway into what I thought was the bathroom, I found that somehow the bathroom had become a flight of stairs.

I felt myself falling through nothingness. Then I landed hard on my tailbone and bounced rapidly, jarringly, from step to step, clear to the bottom. I lay there in shock for probably a couple of minutes before I started breathing again. Then I hollered, "Dan, come here! Dan!"

He appeared at the top of the stairs looking down at me as I lay, stark naked, on the floor below. "What's . . . what the hell?!"

"I've broken my back," I said. I was now calm, even matter-of-fact. "Get me a blanket and call an ambulance. And, for God's sake, bring me something to pee in—I can't move."

I found it amazing that I was not in unbearable pain. From the beginning, I found the whole experience fascinating. Later I was even to feel some gratitude for it because I had been feeling a lot of fear about what would happen to me if I were to become seriously ill or injured. Though my ex-husband, Bob, provided medical insurance for the children, I had none.

X-rays revealed that I had in fact crushed two vertebrae in my lower back. I actually felt a kind of euphoria again and again during my treatment as doctors, nurses, and friends took care of me lovingly. At this late point in my life,

103

I still actually needed to learn how to love and care for others, and I got great instruction from these giving people.

I kept feeling as though I had been cold to everyone all my life—again, with the exception of motherhood. I had passionately adored my babies, unconditionally loving everything about them. This may have been the onset of my spiritual opening to the truth of universal love. Several years later, I heard a minister proclaim that a mother's love is the closest thing to the purity of God's love.

I spent several weeks in bed when I returned home to my apartment. I continued to learn and grow from this experience as I was forced to simply take care of myself, to rest and restore my strength. My friends visited for the long talks I had never had time for before. I even had time to make beautiful, elaborate collage valentines for all of them, and for those who had believed in and supported Telefax. I was struck by how long it had been since I had done any artwork. For several months, I had to wear a back brace everywhere. I found this very humbling.

Dan tried very hard to be there for me. Usually effusively affectionate, he began to withdraw around my injury and convalescence. When he did show up, he was surly and distant. Any encounter with injury and illness brought back the old terror and pain of Vietnam, he told me. I understood but felt I needed more from a partner. Our relationship began to decline and we eventually parted.

On our last date, we attended the opening of the city's new Vietnam Memorial together. It was pouring down rain, but thousands of people were there to see the moving ceremony and visit the beautiful monument, a replica of the Washington wall.

As we filed past the wall, Dan held my hand in a tight grip. We approached a group of people coming from the other direction and Dan made eye contact with a man about his age. They stopped and stared at each other, then suddenly moved together to clutch and hold each other for several moments, both crying. Then, without a word, the man moved on.

"Who was that, Dan?" I asked him. "Did you serve with him?"

He looked at me with deep, tormented anguish in his eyes. His voice was soft and full of pain. "No," he replied, "I never saw him before today."

Something cracked open inside my heart. I was jolted by the realization of the commonality of human experience and human emotion. I clearly saw the Oneness of all human beings in that hug between two grieving men.

I wrote a poem to Dan, expressing my deep feelings about our time together and my frustration with my growing list of "not the one's."

During this four-year spiritual growth period, every day seemed to offer me vitally important lessons for the awakening of my Soul. There were major incidents, such as my fall downstairs, and relationships—like the one with Dan—which taught me compassion and humility. In addition, I began to see and hear revelatory messages all around me.

One day I saw a TV show broadcast by satellite from Russia. It featured a group of ordinary Russian citizens talking about their lives. One woman about my age told how upset she was when her little child came home from kindergarten terrified about the bomb. I was flabbergasted. That woman was me. I had felt the very same thing about my kids. I suddenly felt that my government had deceived me all my life into thinking that the Russians were all evil, conspiring, unfeeling monsters.

I came across a book called *The Supreme Doctrine, Psychological Studies in Zen Thought*. In it I read that positive (usually called good) elements and negative (usually called bad) elements are always neutralized in the energy of something called the conciliatory principle. The balance is

105

essential to life, it said. There is no yin without yang, no light without dark, no valley without mountains. Could it really be possible to just see everything as a necessary part of existence, to stop judging and worrying, to suspend fear? But then, how could we choose anything? Surely there is right and wrong, good and evil? Still, I was intrigued by this concept. I wanted to learn more.

Other books just seemed to show up in my life. They were philosophical or spiritual in nature, and all seemed to me to have the same message: There is a Great Good that is infinite and pure love. It is operating the Universe and all else seen and unseen. We are in it, of it, filled with it, one with it. We can choose to change our consciousness, to unconditionally love ourselves and others. Moreover, the whole world is beginning to see new ways of operating out of these ancient "new" ideas as modern technological advances bring us all together.

106

I slowly began to shift my way of seeing the world. I could feel a beautiful power awakening in me. I sometimes found myself in the euphoric state I had experienced at the end of my three-day First Episode, but it never lasted.

∞

I rearranged the pillows on my hospital bed for sleeping and lay down with a sigh. I selected one of the sleep tapes and snapped it into the Walkman. I felt some sadness about Dan. I sometimes wondered if we had blown a potentially great relationship.

I realized that I had addressed some heavy issues on this Easter Sunday. Yet it was appropriate, I thought, that on this day I had begun to look at my own time of resurrection. I felt certain that during my First Episode, on that winter night in 1985 in the Big House, the Holy Spirit had powerfully moved to awaken me to the Truth, to resurrect my lost relationship with God. This First Episode had been the doorway to the past four years of spiritual growth that had culminated in my stay here on the psych ward, where it was all coming together in the Light.

I was being given many gifts. Some of them were even in material form, I realized as I gratefully placed the headphones of the Walkman over my ears, pushed the button, and drifted off to sleep to the soothing voice of the Walkman angel.

### TO DAN

I hurt inside my body
From collision with carpeted
Sawtooth nightmare plunge,
Step into nothingness,
Jarring, searing, screaming.

I hurt inside my mind
From insult, anger
For an unknown act of
Negligence and ignorance,
Accusation of treason indefensible.

I hurt inside my heart
For love compressed to oblivion.
Fractured, aching empty
Darkness of space forever,
Eternally lost experience of union.

I weep for you.
I assign you to your place
In my lot of markers
For the Special People,
And assign the hurt to my spirit.

SUSAN BREWSTER

NOVEMBER 14, 1986

107

# ELEVEN

# VOLCANOES AND OTHER LESSONS

*We now have many more options about reality, reflected in the many new kinds of social institutions for education.*

—DR. RICHARD ALPERT (RAM DASS), PSYCHOLOGIST

Monday, April 17, 1989—Morning: I woke up with the sobering realization that this was my fifth day on the lockup ward. Sometimes I actually forgot where I was. Perhaps that was because I didn't see it so much as a prison anymore—it seemed more like a healing center. As I had used my time here to review my life, I was also applying this new perspective to my past, healing old hurts as I saw the hurtful incidents in a new way. I again realized that my stay here had a perfect purpose.

The early morning sunlight streaming through my hospital window seemed warmer, more yellow than it had on previous days. After a breakfast of pancakes, I returned to my bed to rest. I saw the Walkman sitting on the nightstand and remembered that my friend, Sandy, had sent me the Easter Service tape from LEC, the church we both loved. I was very excited as I slipped it into the little machine and turned it on.

Nothing could have prepared me for the ecstasy of listening to this service. The music and joyful messages filled my head and heart with bursting awareness of the presence of God in my life. I believed that the same kind of rebirth that had happened to Jesus on that long-ago morning, real or symbolic, was happening to me, right there on that spring morning on the lockup ward. Tears streamed down my face as I listened.

When the tape was over, I lay back against the cool pillows thinking about the wonderful work that was being done at LEC and what a profound difference it had made in my life. This reminded me of the next series of experiences and lessons in the unique part of my life that was the last four years of spiritual growth and discovery. I had learned how to share and function lovingly with a group of people, dealt with some painful family addictions, and found a wonderful church where I felt loved and good, not guilty and bad. I closed my eyes, remembering these exciting events:

110

Soon after my fall downstairs and my breakup with Dan, my broken back began to heal nicely. For a while, however, I was unable to sit at a drafting board so I could not return to architectural design work with Creative Contracting. The girls and I continued living in the apartment. I went to work for my landlord, who owned a number of properties, doing clerical work and some design and construction management.

I felt increasing longing within my Soul. I continued to explore many spiritual paths, looking for Self- and God-realization. The more I read and heard and saw, the more I craved spiritual knowledge and practice.

Many of my most profound experiences were not specifically spiritual, but they taught me clear spiritual values. One of these involved my good friend, Maryanne Griffin. We had been through a lot together, including our respective divorces. Her son, Jason, and my Erik played on the same baseball and ice hockey teams and were best friends.

I remembered how Maryanne and I had met at a Little League game one afternoon. My daughter, Jaqui, had come to watch Erik play, and before the game, she had fallen on the playground and cut her head. A beautiful blonde woman whom I had seen at games before, but never met, had run to her car, crying out that she had a first aid kit. When she returned, I was kneeling on the ground with Jaqui, who lay bleeding and crying. Maryanne knelt beside me and gently soothed my daughter as she cleaned and dressed the cut. I just watched her. I remembered thinking that I had just met a real life angel.

Maryanne and I began to spend time together, and a few months later she encouraged me to attend a personal growth seminar called The Forum, because she believed that it had made a profound difference in her life. I resisted, using money as my reason. Finally, she gave me a scholarship and I attended The Forum—Werner Erhardt's expanded and improved version of EST, a self-discovery and improvement course that became popular in the sixties.

In this training, we learned to tap into authentic personal power. We learned how to do and get what we want, not by intimidating and manipulating others, but by communicating honestly our deepest selves, thereby connecting with them on a whole new level. We learned that living as one's word is essential to living a life of integrity and that who we are is who we say we are.

We began to see the isolationism, apathy, and greed that characterizes a society based on competition—not trust or love—and we saw how we have consequently learned to fear nearly everything and everybody. However clumsily, for it is uncharted territory in American education, this program fostered truly loving group consciousness. It promoted noncompetitive team function, a sense of egalitarianism, and loving regard and union with one's fellow human beings.

The Forum, however, was not without faults. It was a bit pushy, and it was lacking in direct spiritual expression. However, it contributed to my transition from pure intellectualism to spiritual awareness, probably most importantly by giving me a new way of being in authentically loving relationship.

My most vivid experience of this occurred when a number of us who had completed The Forum later attended an advanced seminar called High Performance. There we were put into small teams and instructed on how to create and implement a challenging and meaningful project.

Our team, labeled by the number five, consisted of six people: Todd Hutchinson, a devilish and handsome young attorney; Ron Garst, a biologist; Doug Peterson, a caring speech pathologist; Nancy Goff, a young businesswoman with the face and disposition of an angel; tall, pretty Karen Gorder; and myself. Karen had a Ph.D. in education. She later married Ron and they had a son, Samuel Dakota. Using our new cooperative skills, we instantly bonded into a tight unit. We called ourselves Team Five and we formed a circle of friendship during this experience that has lasted for years.

This team of people and the project we completed together impacted my life tremendously. It was simply my first experience ever of loving, cooperative group functioning. This, to me, is spirituality in its highest form.

I remembered how our project had begun on a very early morning in August 1987. My youngest daughter, Libbi, then fifteen, had been invited to join us:

I shook myself awake, turned off the alarm, then reached over to jostle Libbi, curled up in her sleeping bag next to me. My eyes burned and my body protested the idea of moving from its horizontal position at 4 A.M. We members of Team Five were about to ascend Mt. St. Helens, the active volcano in southern Washington that had erupted a few years before.

"Lib, it's four o'clock. It's time," I whispered.

"Oh God, Mom, you're kidding."

"We've got to get into our gear and meet everyone for breakfast, Hon."

"Right. OK," she muttered, crawling out.

I pulled on a set of long underwear and a red windbreaker, a pair of heavy wool socks and my work boots, and topped it all with a billed cap. I pushed a pair of goggles up on my head in readiness to protect my contact-lensed eyes from glare. Libbi was soon similarly attired and we joined the team at the campground's homey little cafe, which was bustling. We were not the only hungry predawn climbers.

"You made it! Gosh, isn't this cozy?" Nancy Goff hugged us warmly, beaming and gracious even at this hour. Everyone was on time. That was part of our Forum training. We were a diverse, attractive bunch, full of energy and elan. We laughed and jabbered through a delicious breakfast of bacon, country sausage, fluffy omelets, cinnamon rolls, cold juice, and lots of hot coffee.

Later, at the foot of the trail, we donned packs, checked gear, and took photos of us, clean and smiling, arms around each other. Everyone divvied up my gear. This was our agreement as my back was still weak and tender from my fall a few months before.

After we crossed a large field of giant, craggy boulders, the toughest thing was to just keep climbing. The trail was fairly steep, but the worst of it was that it was mostly scree—loose volcanic rocks, mixed with sand. It was like climbing a six-mile sand dune. More than halfway up by noon, we stopped for lunch, settling on some boulders as comfortably as we could. It was a perfect, clear day—warm, but with a nice breeze. The view was already breathtaking. The mountain was stark and bare, yet its vast sweep of gray softness, sloping away far below us, had a unique beauty and grandeur.

I would never forget standing on the edge of the crater of Mt. St. Helens with my daughter and Team Five. We were covered with gray ash, looking somewhat ghoulish, panting and triumphant. One by one, we sank to our knees to rest. We felt respectful, even reverent, as we gazed into the depths of the great volcano.

Clouds would drift across the opening then part dramatically, as if planned by some great theatrical director, to reveal the massive, swelling lava dome with its fissures and steam vents. We could hear avalanches clattering and rumbling from somewhere far across the giant, gaping abyss. Between the avalanches, there was complete stillness. We were likewise silent, feeling awed and humbled. I was feeling a new depth in experiences like these, as though they were somehow awakening my Soul.

114

When we rose, I noticed that my back was beginning to ache and my legs were wobbly. I felt like I was near the limits of my endurance and looked forward to an easier descent. Going down turned out to be even harder on my body and back than climbing. Several grueling hours later, we came out on level ground. I was near collapse for the remaining mile, weak and rubber-legged, having to rest every few yards.

I never felt a moment of regret for my suffering that day. I knew that climbing Mt. St. Helens was somehow far more than just a physical accomplishment for me. I had found a new way to relate to people, a new form of family—and this, too, was part of my awakening spiritual Self.

The years 1987 and 1988 continued to be a period of growing awareness for me. Because it still felt foreign and somehow threatening, I sometimes tried to control my mounting spiritual energy with a strong mind. I had no idea how to surrender to anything. Though basically loving, I was still lacking in humility. I hadn't become reacquainted with God on a personal level, and I didn't know how to access my spiritual side in everyday struggles.

Sometime during this period, I accompanied my daughter, Jaqui, to a "quit smoking" program. I was not ready to give up smoking myself—I was there only to support her, I told everyone. However, the message was so convincing that I have never smoked another cigarette since then. I learned a lot about addiction in that program. I learned how strong and intelligent Jaqui is, and how committed to Good. I had always found it difficult to admit I was wrong or to let others show me a better way. In this program, I learned a little more humility and expanded the ability I had acquired after breaking my back to ask for and receive help from others.

Also during this time, I began attending some Adult Children of Alcoholics (ACOA) meetings with Sandy, my good friend from architecture school. My father and my ex-husband were both practicing alcoholics. ACOA is a twelve-step support group program patterned after Alcoholics Anonymous (AA). It was at ACOA meetings that I heard the freeing phrase, "Let go and let God."

After a few meetings, I was devastated to have to face the fact that my whole childhood and marriage had been pervaded with the effects of the disease of alcoholism. I learned that many of the behaviors and family dynamics that characterized these areas of my life were destructive. At first, I translated that to mean that my whole life, which I had considered normal, had been distorted. This produced a kind of identity crisis. I felt I needed to begin life all over again with a different set of parameters and values.

Initially, I saw no other way to do this than to reject my parents and all they represented and to see my entire marriage as a failure. I wished to preserve my family relationships, however, and I even felt that I could help my family by sharing my new ideas, no matter how difficult that might

115

be at first. Moreover, I could see many wonderful things about my marriage—including my children. Eventually, I began to understand and forgive my parents and Bob, recognizing the fears and hurts that were underlying their behaviors as my own in different forms.

I attended ACOA meetings regularly for a number of months. I mostly listened at first, feeling apart and superior. Gradually, I learned that when I spoke my truth, tentatively and woodenly at first, I felt a strange warmth. Among these people I sensed the comradeship and commonality for which I had longed my entire life.

In spite of all these new and enriching experiences, I continued to feel confused and dissatisfied. I was still mystified by my First Episode, wondering if the euphoria that followed it had any relationship to the states of enlightenment I was reading about. I still suffered from insomnia.

116

Sometime in mid-1988, I visited a friend in Seattle and attended a Unity Church with her. I was astounded at how similar the ideas I heard there were to all my recent reading, to Forum concepts, and to twelve-step ideas. I learned that Unity Church focused on the Bible, particularly on Jesus' teachings of Love and Forgiveness, yet it embraced and accepted all faiths and all ideologies, just as I was continuing to discover how much alike all people really are. This seemed very aligned with my newly emerging spiritual values.

The minister at the Seattle Unity Church hugged me as we left that Sunday. It was a wonderful feeling. When I told her where I was from, she asked warmly, ""Have you heard about LEC, the Living Enrichment Center?"

"Um, I think some of the folks at ACOA have mentioned it," I replied.

"It's really supposed to be a dynamic, wonderful church," she said.

This visit to Seattle Unity Church was not how I remembered my few childhood church experiences. On the two-hundred-mile drive home, I felt warm and loved and loving all the way. Two weeks later, I attended LEC for the first time. From that first Sunday, I was drawn to it like a magnet:

LEC was held in a suburban movie theater at this time. I was amazed to see hundreds of people pouring through the lobby where the smell of popcorn still hung in the air. I felt the warm, excited energy, almost like a tangible thing, as I mingled with the crowd, entered the theater, and took a seat. I noticed that the minister here, as at Seattle Unity, was a woman.

"Good morning!" the minister called out from the center of the softly lit stage.

Over a thousand voices responded, "Good morning!"

"Let's celebrate God's presence together. Let's stand, recognizing there is one presence, one power in this universe. And that presence and power we call God. It's with us, it's for us, and it's within us right now. Let's celebrate."

I was transfixed, not so much by what this woman was saying as by the soft timbre and melodic elegance of her voice. It seemed to burst rapturous, angelic, motherly, and overpowering all at once, from some place deep, deep inside her being.

We stood and sang: "The only thing in all my life is knowing you, loving you, serving you." Something poignantly familiar like a memory of some beautiful, long lost home wafted through my mind. I rarely cried. It stuffed up my sinuses. I hated feeling out of control, but I could not stop the tears from running down my face. Fortunately, I was not the only one. Apparently crying was a part of this song, or this place, or something.

The song ended and everyone sat. The rustling stilled, and heads were bowed. The minister led a prayer: "Thank you, God, for the gift of this day, a new beginning, an unopened gift you have set before us. Our prayer today is

117

for a new willingness to listen to you, to really listen to you, as the voice of divine wisdom and guidance, unconditional love. Through that still small voice you speak to us individually. We pray today for a new willingness. Amen."

I was surprised. I had never heard a prayer more articulate or sensible. Pray for a new willingness? What exactly did she mean? Was that enough? Was that possible? The idea was exciting to me, the words as beautiful as the tiny, shining woman who spoke them. Mary Manin Morrissey was the spiritual leader of this progressive church. I learned it was part of a worldwide network of churches representing a movement called "New Thought," which, like Unity, accepted all faiths, all religions, all beliefs as valid and commonly sourced by one living God.

I was filled with joy and intense hope as I left LEC that first Sunday. I felt again the euphoria of my three-day First Episode, and it lasted for several days. I wasn't sure what was causing it, but it was clearly linked with my experience at that church.

All my intellectual resistance arose by late in the following week. I was sure I had just responded to group hysteria. I felt some fear that I was being controlled by some religious fanatic fervor, but I could not deny that certain intangible changes happened in my life that week: I felt generally happier, and life seemed easier; people seemed more troubled than evil to me; I worried less; my anxiety eased, and I slept better.

It never occurred to me that I had found my Spiritual Path. I certainly did not recognize "a new willingness" in my decision to return to LEC to hear more that next Sunday—and the next and the next and the next. As the Sundays came and went, I became more comfortable with the concept of God, talking the talk with increasing ease, but the concrete effects in my day-to-day life during the rest of the week seemed marginal. I couldn't see that the outside world was conforming quickly enough to the new ideas being taught at LEC to save it—or me.

Nevertheless, I followed this new path with increasing fascination and enthusiasm. I learned to meditate. I continued to work on letting go and letting God. I learned to be accountable in situations where I used to blame and feel guilty. I tried very hard to learn to pray.

I longed to change my life, to be more orderly, more serene, more loving, more serving, more forgiving. Yet I still thought it was really about other people, other countries, other bosses, other boyfriends, other children. If only they would change, if only they would all come to LEC, everything would work out fine.

Something still lay dormant in me. I had visited and observed it and danced around its sleeping form. I knew it was there, and I knew it could live in me and give me what I wanted. I knew it was awake in others. I even knew that the choice to awaken it was really mine. I thought I didn't know how, but I guess I just wasn't ready. For some reason, I was still afraid to let the Holy Spirit awaken me, afraid of what some people would think if I were like that, afraid of my own goodness, afraid of God. I continued to try to intellectualize it all. I had a long and powerful personal and cultural history in this method of processing.

119

I noticed that I felt like crying again. This was getting to be a real habit here on the psych ward, but it seemed like a good habit. It felt so good. I realized that there was a shift happening in the feelings behind the tears. When I had thought about all the painful events of my earlier life, the tears had been caused by a lot of pent-up frustration, rage, and pain. As I progressed through the memories of the last four years, I noticed that there was increasing joy and relief behind the tears.

I got up and walked to the window. I stood gazing out on the freeway, letting the soft morning sun warm my face and dry my tears. I knew that I was experiencing a miracle here—a miracle of rebirth—and I was grateful.

# TWELVE

# CHALLENGES

*A final kind of difficulty may confront the individual during periods in which the flow of superconscious energies is growing easier and more abundant. This energy flow may either be scattered in feverish activity or may be kept too much in abeyance, unexpressed, so that it accumulates high pressure, which can even cause physical problems.*

—Dr. Roberto Assagioli, Psychiatrist

Monday, April 17, 1989—Afternoon: I watched in horror as two attendants wheeled a woman off the ward in a wheelchair. I had been told that they took her every day for electric shock treatments. She looked young, like my short-term roommate, Margaret. I wondered how Margaret was doing. This young woman just sat in the chair, her head lolling to one side, her eyes vacant.

I became fascinated with the whole concept of mental illness during my stay at the psych ward. I realized that being a patient there, no matter what the reason, was an experience that could not be contrived by psychology students, no matter how dedicated they were. I saw it as a remarkable opportunity to learn firsthand about that most dreaded of all processes, worse even than death, called losing your mind.

I eventually concluded that there was no such thing. I became convinced by my experience there that every patient on that ward had constant thoughts and felt joy, fear, and pain like everybody else. It seemed to me that it was all caused by stimuli that were arranged in patterns foreign to other minds. Of course, when it manifested in behaviors that interrupted their lives, these people obviously needed treatment, but it seemed as though the treatment could be a lot more sensitive.

Whatever the cause of my symptoms, they sometimes felt enough like mental illness that I was able to relate to the lost world of the other patients on the ward. Whether it was the medications or duress or spiritual awakening, there were times, for example, when my short-term memory did not function properly. I found this terrifying, which made it worse. I was told to make lists and not to worry about it. For a woman who had survived by excelling in mental acumen, it was an amazing and unforgettable lesson in humility.

122

I had written a little list of visitors for this day. My current boyfriend, Jack Durant, was coming this afternoon. Dear friend, Sandy Sonksen, would visit this evening. I was really looking forward to seeing Sandy—not so much, Jack. He was just another in a long line of "not the one's." Noticing this disparity in my feelings, I realized that I still felt toward men a cynicism that needed healing.

Jack Durant and I had been in a steady but rocky relationship for several months. He was an architect, and I had met him at a business function. He arrived to visit after lunch. As usual, the first thing I did when I saw him was evaluate his looks and demeanor. He was energetic and I was attracted to his stocky, muscular body, but I had often found him quite sexist and controlling.

We had a nice chat. I told him what had been happening to me and reassured him that I was going to be fine, that in fact I expected to be discharged within a day or two and needed him to pick me up. He said he would. It was interesting how detached we were in spite of how constant his presence and involvement had been in my past month of remarkable, distressing experiences. It seemed that he, like everyone else, just couldn't understand how intense it all was for me.

After Jack left, I fluffed my pillows and lay back, sinking into them and thinking about how seeing him had reminded me of the next phase of my four-year growth period. During our relationship, I had encountered some traumatic health issues—one of mine and one of my daughter, Jaqui's—which had given me opportunities for more spiritual development. I closed my eyes, remembering this time:

∞

During the late fall of 1988 and early winter of 1989, Jack and I had been in a committed relationship. We had decided to share a huge studio space in a wonderful old refurbished warehouse in the city's developing art district. Jack set up part of the space as a classroom where he planned to teach a course he had created to help people contract the building of their own homes.

Our relationship, like all my relationships, cycled through extreme ups and downs. At one point, I had moved into Jack's apartment, then out again within a couple of weeks. At Christmastime, I found myself living at the studio for a month to save money for an apartment of my own. Libbi, in her last year of high school, was temporarily staying with a friend, planning to share the apartment with me.

One night during this time, just before Christmas, I dealt with a physical crisis that evoked new awareness and insight:

I had been out for the evening and, upon returning alone to the studio, was feeling mounting terror about an unusual growth on my breast, which I had discovered only that morning. I reached for the phone. My hand trembled so violently, I could hardly push the buttons. I dialed Dr. Ryan's office and asked that she call me at once. It was nearly

123

midnight. A few minutes later, Barbara Ryan's husband, Dr. Tom Ryan, called me back.

"Susan? Is this Susan Brewster?"

"Yes. This is she. I need to speak to Barbara."

"She's out of town at a conference, Susan. Can I help you with something?"

"Well, Tom, maybe you can. I have a large growth on my breast. I just woke up with it this morning. It is like a huge boil, about half an inch in diameter, but it doesn't really hurt. I went to the theater tonight with some old friends. One of them, Mark Hanson, is an ob/gyn doctor. I asked him if he would mind looking at this thing before we went to the theater." I paused and took a deep breath, then rushed on. "When he saw it, Tom, he said he thought it might be a form of cancer. I've been petrified all evening. I couldn't even tell you what the play was. I—I feel like I need a second opinion, so I wanted to talk to Barbara. Sorry to call so late, I'm just so upset."

There was complete silence on the other end of the phone line for several seconds.

"Dr. Ryan?"

"Uh . . . yes, yes. Well," I could hear the caution and concern in his voice, "I certainly shouldn't question another physician without seeing you," he said, "but it could be so many things. If you had cancer that was erupting in that way, it seems to me it would have become apparent by now with other symptoms. It could be just a topical problem, a blocked pore or something. Can you come in first thing in the morning?"

"Of course," I said. "Uh, Tom, can I ask you one thing?"

"Sure."

"Are you saying that I definitely don't have anything serious? I don't have cancer?"

"I can't rule out anything without seeing you, but it doesn't sound like it to me from what you're telling me."

"Thanks, Tom, thanks a lot."

I hung up the phone. I felt much better, but I still had a nagging doubt. After all, Mark Hanson was a respected physician. As I thought more about it, the little doubt turned back into a terror that gripped me all night long. On this night, the huge building was empty. No one else lived there; it was not zoned for residential use. I had never felt more alone.

I wanted to call someone, but it was so late, and I didn't want to bother anybody. I crawled into my sleeping bag and just allowed the thoughts and feelings to surface. I thought about what I would do if it turned out to be cancer and I really was dying. I decided that, if it was cancer, I knew exactly what had caused it. It was a lifetime of repressing pain and resentment and fear. I thought about how I would convey this to everyone, to perhaps help them.

I especially thought of how this could be an opportunity to teach my children that disease is truly *dis-ease*, and that it wasn't too late for them to learn healthier behaviors. I was very concerned about my children. I had been so confused lately. I knew I had not consciously taught them the new values I had been learning, and I was afraid that they would be unreceptive to spiritual ideas.

I had believed that I had created open and honest relationships with my children. Yet I learned from time to time that they had secret issues. Nothing disturbed me more than to learn that they had tried to struggle with fear and pain alone. This should not have surprised me. It is exactly what I had learned to do. And it is what their father learned to do. Isn't that what we all learned in this society? Isn't that its very cornerstone—individual strength and achievement, self-reliance, and self-control?

My thoughts turned to some issues that I had helped Jaqui deal with a few months before. It all began one evening when Jaqui and Libbi and I still lived together. On

125

this particular evening, Jaqui was home, Libbi was out, and my youngest son, Erik, had come over to stay with us:

Erik, my dimpled, fair-haired darling, was to face his own alcohol issues years later, but on this night he was concerned about his sister. He came and sat near me as I watched TV in the living room. Jaqui was in her room. For a few minutes he just watched the show on television, then suddenly turned to me. "Mom, there's something I want to talk to you about."

I could tell it was something serious. "What is it, Er?"

"Umm, I'm sort of afraid to tell you. I think Jaqui will get mad at me."

"I see," I said carefully. "Well, it's up to you."

"I think you ought to know about this though," he looked at the floor.

126

"Well, then maybe you'd better tell me and let Jaqui have her feelings anyway," I encouraged, growing a little concerned now.

"Go ask her if I can tell you," he said quickly.

"How can I ask her if I don't know what it is?"

"Just go ask her. She'll know."

I walked to Jaqui's door and knocked.

"Yes?" she called out.

"Can I come in and ask you something?"

"Sure."

I opened the door and walked into her room. She lay curled on her bed surrounded by stuffed animals. She was writing a letter and listening to her Walkman. I noticed how much she had matured this year. She was really a woman, a pretty, perky little woman. Her long strawberry blond hair framed her freckled face. She tired of being called a Sissy Spacek look-alike. She looked up at me with huge, round blue eyes, pulling off the headset.

"Erik says there is something he wants to tell me. I guess it's about you, because he says he is afraid you'll be upset if he does. He told me to come and ask you if he can tell me." I was sure my voice conveyed my confusion.

She just looked at me for several long seconds, then shrugged. I could tell she wasn't going to say more. I returned to the living room and told Erik he could tell me. By now, I was going to hear this thing one way or another.

"Well, Jaqui has been throwing up after she eats. I hear her. So does Libbi. Libbi says she has been doing it for a long time and I'm scared."

I stared at him. The symptoms of bulimia and anorexia were common knowledge to teenagers and their parents these days, as social pressure to be model slim had reached insane proportions. A symptom of which I had been unaware was about to become known to me, however—the extreme secrecy which most bulimics utilize to deny and protect their behavior.

I went to Jaqui's room and said calmly, "Come out. We have to talk about this."

127

She flew out of her room, turned up the volume on the TV and plopped down angrily on the couch to watch it. I slowly walked to the television, turned it off, and faced her. "We have a lot of options, Jaqui, but not talking about it isn't one of them."

Within a week, her father and I had sponsored her entering an eating disorders program, but I was dismayed. I had really believed that I had good communication with my children. This made me question that.

During this time of Jaqui's recovery, she was working for Nancy Goff, my good friend from Team Five, with whom I had climbed Mt. St. Helens. One day, Nancy called me at work. "Susan, something is terribly wrong with Jaqui. She can't stop crying. She wants you to come and get her."

I went and picked her up. We went home and I held her while she just cried and sobbed for three or four hours. We didn't speak a word. She just cried as though she'd pulled the cork on a giant container of liquid pain. I remember thinking that I hadn't seen her cry since she was a very little girl. I also realized that I almost never cried with my children. I felt that I had to be strong. I had realized at that moment that it takes incredible strength and courage to be vulnerable and honest enough to cry.

Glancing around the studio, I noticed that the atmosphere was almost eerie. Jack and I had set up a Christmas tree and the lights cast a glow like firelight in the cavernous room.

I thought about what was going on currently in my own life. I was forty-four years old. I had been divorced for eleven years and had not been able to create a committed relationship with a man. I knew that I wanted to marry again. Obviously, some fear was keeping me from it. I was working for a large, successful remodeling company, designing kitchens and additions. I earned commissions on fifteen to seventy thousand dollar contracts, but I never had enough money to feel secure and successful. I alternated between being terrified of my tyrannical boss and vociferously defying and challenging him, my usual pattern with authoritarian men. The pressure was terrific. And I was not expressing my artist nature nearly enough. I was not happy, not at peace, not fulfilled.

As if all that were not enough, apparently even my relationships with my children, always a stabilizing factor for me, were in question, not to mention that my body seemed to be falling apart.

True, I had heard and read and experienced many new ideas about a loving God, about the Divine Order of the universe and how I could access the living Christ within me when I needed strength and comfort. But all of this seemed ineffectual when I was facing a real issue. I bought it because it made sense to me and it felt good, but that mysterious state called Faith eluded me. I talked the talk, but my deepest Self did not hear it.

128

Finally, completely engulfed in self-doubt and terror, I said a halfhearted little prayer and fell into a restless sleep.

The following morning, Dr. Ryan confirmed that I had some kind of an external abscess. He lanced and drained it and it healed in a short time.

∞

I felt sad thinking about those dark times. I could see now how lost my children had become as well. I didn't know if there was anything I could do to help them when I got out of this hospital. It seemed as if I might have missed my chance; they were all virtually adults. But I knew that I would try, that I would never stop loving them and trying to serve them in the role of their mother, their guide, their teacher.

I heard a commotion in the hall. They were returning the young woman in the wheelchair to her room. I hoped and prayed that they knew what they were doing, that the shock treatments were helping her. She looked exactly the same to me, but I knew there were things in this world that I didn't understand. I had to learn to trust—to trust others, to trust myself, and above all, to trust the Great Good, the organizing energy of this beautiful existence, the energy that I was learning to call God.

# THIRTEEN

# THE ROSE WINDOW

*Our world of seeing, hearing, smelling, tasting or touching
starts to dissolve. With this comes a great sense of unease
and fear, even an experience of terror. Not only is the outer
world dissolving, but the inner world as well and we lose
our entire sense of reference. At this point there can arise
very powerful visions.*

—DR. JACK KORNFIELD, BUDDHIST MONK AND
PSYCHOLOGIST

131

Monday, April 17, 1989—Evening: I was overjoyed
to see Sandy Sonksen, my dearest friend from
architecture school. "God, Sue, you really know how to get
my attention!" she joked. "Seriously," she said, "I had no
idea it was like this, Sue. I guess that's what you were trying
to tell us all. I just didn't get it. I didn't understand!" She
had tears in her eyes.

"It's OK, Sandy. I didn't know how to convey it to you.
And it isn't 'like this.' I don't really belong here. They don't
understand either," I told her. I felt exasperated all over
again. "Anyway, you're here. Sit down and I'll tell you all
about it. I've been realizing the most amazing things about
my life. I believe this is all being directed by God, Sandy."

She sat. I told her. She understood at last. One of the
things I loved most about Sandy was that she treated me
with great respect— as though what I had to say was always

valid and important. She just looked at me for a long time. "My God, Sue, it sounds like you are having some kind of spiritual crisis. Has anyone seen that here?"

"No way," I responded. "*Spiritual* isn't part of the vocabulary here. I even went to a religion group led by a nun. She urged us to pray and have faith in God. I had no argument there, but when I asked her if awakening to God could be mentally disturbing, she said, 'God works in mysterious ways, Dear.' She had no answers and didn't want to hear about my experiences. She was as patronizing as the rest of them here."

Sandy frowned and tsk'd sympathetically. "Did you get the tape from Easter service?"

"Oh yes, Sandy. I can't thank you enough. It was incredible!"

We talked for two more hours. After she left, I lay back on the bed to ponder. I felt so lucky to have wonderful, close friends. Suddenly I realized that I had developed most of them in the past four years. It was almost as though it was all part of the plan for my spiritual awakening. My friends had been instrumental in my seeing this breakdown as a breakthrough. They had all come through for me when I cried out to them, when things got really intense.

I knew it was time to think about the final stages, the climax of my spiritual crisis, my horrifying and glorious Second Episode. I closed my eyes, remembering how it had begun—just a few weeks ago in early March:

∞

I had moved out of the studio at last as Libbi and I had found a wonderful apartment in an old Victorian house. It had twelve-foot ceilings, velvety green carpet, and, in the living room, a huge bay window and a pretty marble fireplace.

For several years Libbi had been happily attending a remarkable public alternative school I had discovered while doing a college paper on art education. It was a loving, progressive school with no tests, no grades, no cheerleaders or football team.

I had been working for a large, upscale remodeling company for a couple of years. I was designing high-end kitchens, bathrooms, and additions. Money had gotten better, and I was healthy and generally much more content than I had been before Christmas—or so I thought. Suddenly one morning, I was struck by a heinous, debilitating illness:

I awoke with crushing pressure threatening to explode my head. My throat felt like someone had ripped out my tongue. Every particle of my body smoldered with the heat of high fever. I slipped a burning foot out of the sheets, feeling the immediate coolness of the morning air, and let it fall heavily to the green carpeted floor. I could hear Libbi clattering in the kitchen. She was either making her breakfast or packing her lunch to take to school.

I could not make my body follow my foot. I called out to her, "Lib, Hon, can you call work and tell them I'm sick?"

She came and leaned a forearm against the carved jamb of the bedroom doorway. "What's wrong, Mom?"

"I don't know. Flu, I guess. I feel like I'm dying." I rarely got even a cold. I didn't have time to be sick. I had never felt anything like this before.

For the next two weeks, hellish symptoms gripped my body and mind with voracious tenacity. I lost in totality my senses of taste and smell, and my head was so stuffed up that I could hardly hear at times. I was so weak and depleted that I could only lie in bed, day after endless day.

I called Dr. Ryan's office. The nurse said there was still late flu around; it was viral, and there was really nothing to do for it but rest and take aspirin.

Jack and I still shared the studio just a few blocks from the new apartment. I called him for support. He sounded

133

cool and even irritated. I was profoundly hurt, then furious at his lack of sympathy for me in my distress and helplessness. What the hell was wrong with men anyway? Were they all insensitive jerks who completely lacked nurturing empathy—or just the ones I picked?

I had never experienced an illness even remotely like this, and the worst part was the mental anguish. By the second week, I was nearly mad with just lying in bed worrying about missing work and every other thing. I couldn't even read. I lost all track of time. I would sleep at all different hours, never very well.

All I could do was lie there and think until it seemed that I had thought about everything in my entire conscious world, then everything retrievable from my subconscious, then everything in the universe. I thought until it felt like my brain was drained, exhausted, devoid of energy.

At the end of two weeks, my body finally began, ponderously, to regain a modicum of vitality. Then suddenly one morning I experienced a mild attack of the electric sensations I had felt four years before. Later that day, the cold shock waves began coursing through my body and paralyzing my legs in the same way that they had done long ago in the Big House. I was mortified at the onset of these dreaded tremors.

This physical state was frightening, but I was simultaneously entering into some kind of bizarre mental state that distressed me even more. It was similar to what had happened four years before, but this time it often felt as though I had crossed a line into a distinctly different reality. Moreover, it seemed that there was an exact moment that I crossed over, and from that moment on, I remained terrified that I would never be able to cross back—though I always did return.

I simply couldn't believe it was all happening again, just like four years ago in the Big House—only much, much worse!

On the second day of these disturbing new occurrences, I managed to trudge weakly into the living room to see if a change of environment would make a difference. A storm with heavy rain and winds pounded and gusted outside. The house was dark and chilly. I sat cross-legged on the couch, facing the bay window, wrapped in a soft wool blanket like a mummy. For several minutes, I just watched the rain run down the glass sections of the lower windows.

Suddenly, I felt compelled to look up at the top part of the middle section of the window, which was stained glass in a beautifully crafted rose pattern. As I watched it, I felt a strange sensation—as though warm water were flowing slowly through my body, beginning at the top of my head. Then I was astonished to notice that the window seemed to be getting brighter. Within a minute or two, it glowed far more brightly than any other part of the window, brighter by far than anything else in the room. It was as though it alone was illuminated from behind.

135

I brushed my eyes with my hand and looked again. It shone even more intensely. I began trembling. I slipped off the couch to the carpeted floor and sat, or rather kneeled there. I left the blanket on the couch as I was suddenly very warm. I gazed, transfixed, at the window. My eyes seemed to be held there by some magnetic power. Without realizing it, I pressed my hands together in a gesture of prayer.

I stared at the luminescent carmine roses with their green leaves and twining blue ribbons for a very long time. The image seemed to radiate to my core, driving out all the weariness, misery, and fear that had accumulated and penetrated every cell. I felt serene, euphoric. I felt I had received some mysterious promise. I found myself whispering a prayer of thanks—for what, I was not sure. I just knew I felt better, different. Then a fear thought entered my mind, and the spell was broken. The window was once again dull.

Returning to bed, I was positive that I was now hallucinating. This potentially comforting experience simply deepened the horror of my growing certainty that I was really losing my mind this time. Later that afternoon, the electric sensations seized my body for nearly half an hour, the longest an attack had ever lasted. I suddenly felt an old terror—that I was going to die. Then I felt a new and overwhelming feeling—that I could not be alone.

It was difficult for my family to come. My mother and sister lived in California at this time, my father lived in the next town, and my children were busy teenagers. However, I had my close friends. Most of them had already been visiting and caring for me during my illness. I was beginning to feel concerned that I was intruding in their lives, but I desperately hoped I could count on their continued support.

I mentally reviewed my support network: There was Sandy Sonksen, my friend from architecture school; Maryanne Griffin, whom I had met on a playground years ago; Alan Jones, my dear friend from design class at college; and then, of course, there was Team Five, with whom I had climbed Mt. St. Helens. With the electric waves and terror mounting again, I called them all. I even called my current, unpredictable boyfriend, Jack, with whom I had broken up for the jillionth time the week before.

I was especially eager to talk to Maryanne's new husband, Rob Wentz, about this latest mental stuff. Drawn to Rob's passionate spirit, I had become close to him. Rob was a former cop who, after watching his partner get shot in the head, had flipped out and been given a psychological discharge. Continuing to suffer, he sometimes raged out of control. He was eventually treated for manic depression. On medication he was his old wonderful self, displaying his brilliant and beautiful Soul. He had spent many hours studying his disease. He was a devoted lover of God and all things spiritual. I knew that God was his supreme resource for his healing work and that he would not be dismayed or upset by any of the shocking things that were presenting themselves to me, including the glowing window.

Everyone I called was surprised to hear the panic and upset in my voice. They all had thought I was getting better. "I don't know what's the matter with me," I told Sandy. "I'm having anxiety attacks again, and I have weird thoughts. Today I became mesmerized or something by my stained glass window. I just feel so incomprehensibly frightened. I feel like I have to have people around me, and Libbi has taken care of me so much. . . . Is there any time you could come over and just be with me for a little while?"

I felt like a weak, whining, helpless invalid. I had tried to tough this thing through by myself, not wanting to be a bother to anyone. I felt that I should be able to just stop it— whatever it was. I had always been able to take care of myself, to solve any problem with my wits and strength of mind.

It was my mental condition that I found the most devastating. My mind was everything to me. I had learned at a very early age that without my mind, I would not be smart and so would not be lovable. I could not imagine what else could be causing me to experience a different reality if I weren't losing my mind. Yet I never felt totally out of touch. I always felt sane, always knew exactly what was happening around me—and within me. That was the oddest part of all.

And so my friends came. Libbi was there at night, but I felt I needed someone during the day. They set up a schedule so someone would be there almost all the time. On that first day, several of them came at once and they decided to call my doctor, Barbara Ryan. Sandy got the number from my book and dialed it.

"Dr. Ryan, this is Sandy Sonksen. I'm a friend of Susan Brewster's. She is having a tough time. She is feeling very anxious. She feels that she needs to have someone with her every moment, that something terrible is happening to her."

137

Dr. Ryan told Sandy that I would be fine, that I was lucky to have many loving friends. She prescribed Xanax for my anxiety. The Xanax helped me a great deal. I was able to feel quite calm and rational for periods of time, especially right after taking the pill. But when no one was with me, when I was alone in the house, the terror would return. Though muted, it still gripped me with paralyzing force.

During one such interval, I decided, tentatively, to try accessing the powerful, peaceful state induced previously by the stained glass window. Making sure the shades on all the other windows were drawn so no one could see me, I knelt on the carpet facing the rose window and gazed at it intently. To my amazement, it slowly began to glow again as before. It grew brighter and brighter exactly as if someone were turning on a light behind it with a rheostat. It became so bright it actually seemed to vibrate and shimmer like heat waves above a hot pavement.

138

I was filled with the same rapturous peace as before. And, as before, after some indeterminate length of time, I began wondering what other people would think if they saw me, especially if the window looked normal to them, as doubtlessly it would. I became filled with the certainty that I was hallucinating, that all of this was further proof of my mental instability. The light went out.

Suddenly, another new insight began to dawn deep inside me: I knew I had created that experience of Light and Peace. I had created it and then let it go. If it was madness, I had not stayed there. I had gone there and come back— at will.

I became intensely curious about this euphoric altered state and about my ability to access it at will. The most perplexing thing about it was that it felt strangely familiar— almost like returning home after a long absence. It was the same way I had felt on my first Sunday at LEC. Could it be that this feeling somehow represented a wonderful reality, like a sort of heaven? Was it possible that my competitive, materialistic life of misery and death and anger and fear was a living hell? And, most astoundingly, did I really have the power to choose and create where I wanted to be?

Somehow, intuitively, I knew I was approaching a deep and profound mystical knowledge, a fundamental Truth of Love and Light. It seemed to me that this knowledge could free me, and perhaps all human beings, forever.

I glanced at the window of my hospital room. I realized how many insights I had experienced at that window the last few days. From it, I had enjoyed the new, yellow spring sun and several glorious sunsets. On Easter Sunday I had discovered that I could see the cross atop the tower. And every day I silently related to countless unknown loved ones in the cars speeding along the Eastside Freeway. Suddenly I had a revelation: I knew, in a flash of insight and understanding, that windows symbolized the accessing of the Light—Spiritual Awakening. Now I knew why they put stained glass windows in churches. It was one of those obvious Truths that we see all our lives and don't see.

I lay back and closed my eyes, knowing that I would sleep again tonight. I felt loved and loving.

139

# FOURTEEN

# MIRACLES IN A SILVER CLOUD

*People in spiritual emergency need a particular kind of support. They need support to surrender to higher transpersonal levels.*

—DR. EMMA BRAGDON, PSYCHOLOGIST

Tuesday, April 18, 1989—Morning: I was informed that I would be meeting with the discharge committee this morning. I was a little nervous, but my old self-confidence was coming back. I knew I could impress them with my mind, which was not only sane, but also as facile as ever.

At 9 A.M., I walked with an attendant down the hall to the meeting room where other patients and I had attended exercise group and religion group. We had no other therapy. Apparently the staff believed that most of the patients here were not capable of responding to regular psychotherapy. Two men and Dr. Laura Tanner were sitting in the room waiting for me. The attendant introduced me to them, but not they to me, then left, closing the door.

"Good morning, Ms. Brewster," Dr. Tanner greeted me. She seemed as stiff and detached as ever. She expressed no compassion or concern for the fact that I had just spent five days of my life locked up on a mental ward. This panel of what I assume were doctors asked me a number of questions, including that old standby, "Can you tell us who is the president of the United States?" I answered them all calmly and, I was certain, accurately. Still without a smile or a friendly word, Dr. Tanner said, "Thank you, Ms. Brewster. You may go now."

I went back to my room and lay down on my bed to think. Why does everyone seem so cold here? I wondered. I guess they're just afraid, and I guess that doesn't really make them so different from the patients. Is it really any different here on the psych ward from what it is out there? I wondered, glancing out the window through the bars at the blue sky. For some reason, I was reminded of an exercise we had done in The Forum where we closed our eyes and imagined ourselves among strangers. After a time, we all began to cry from the feelings of isolation and fear. We had realized that most of us have no idea how much fear runs us.

Perhaps, I thought, my fellow patients are people just like me who did not have my resources when they crossed that line. They have been labeled mentally ill, but maybe that means that they are simply those who have most deeply forgotten who they really are. Maybe Dr. Tanner is afraid of what Freud called transference, I thought, because people must continually affirm who they are by mirroring one another, and if we interact with someone who has forgotten who they are, then we may lose ourselves—a terrifying prospect.

I was learning that I could heal my fear by remembering my real God Self. Inevitably, this led to my feeling a strong desire to help others. Moreover, I saw that the most challenging job of a healer is to help people remember that they are sane, beautiful, and Divine. Suddenly, I had a vision of redesigning all the mental wards in the world. I would make them soft and homey. There would be beautiful music and books and art everywhere. There would be classes in loving, spiritual unity—whether or not they seemed to be understood. There would be massage therapists specially trained in gentle techniques to help the patients return to their bodies. There would be puppies and kittens for everyone to love, and children's voices, children's energy and innocence and sweetness all over the place.

I smiled and felt warm all over at this picture of what it could have been like here. Actually, I thought, that would be a nice, healing world to live in anywhere.

This reminded me of the next series of extraordinary events, which occurred during my Second Episode. I had been transported to a nurturing, loving environment and had found God there—in a Silver Cloud. I closed my eyes, remembering:

∞

By early April, after several days of taking medication and being supported by friends, I had felt strong enough to return to work. It felt really good to be back and I had a pile of leads to attack. I called one of them, a woman named Judy Guardino, and set up what I thought was a routine appointment—but this would turn out to be a very significant conversation:

"Is this Judy Guardino?"

"Yes."

"This is Susan Brewster. I'm a designer. You called about remodeling your kitchen?"

"Oh, yes."

"I'd love to help you with that. When would you like to get together? Would an afternoon later this week work for you?"

"Let's see . . . I'm very busy working on the Jesuit auction. My son goes there. Uh . . . checking my calendar . . . uh . . . how about next Monday afternoon, about one o'clock?"

"That would be fine. Good luck with your auction. I'll see you in a week then."

"Thank you so much. I'm looking forward to meeting you. Bye now."

143

I seemed to be handling work capably, but I was afraid it was far from over for me. My body was much better, and I could cope and function with the aid of Xanax, but I sensed that all the mental and emotional turmoil had just been stifled behind a wall of drugs. Oddly, I felt that some vital process had been blocked. It felt so similar to the events of four years ago. And somehow I knew that this time I would not be able to keep it contained.

For a day or two, I had made calls and been able to smile and appear normal at work. One morning as I sat in my private office with the door closed, I began to tremble, and then the cold electric impulses began to travel throughout my body. It had come back, drugs or no.

I called Maryanne at work. She was sympathetic and responsive. "Listen, I'm going to come and get you."

"No, no. I'll probably be OK. I just needed to hear your voice."

144

"Susan, I know you. You wouldn't call if it weren't serious. I'm coming over there right now. I want you to come and stay with us for a couple of days. Robbie is working at home this week. Please come over and let us take care of you, just for a couple of days. We want to, really. It'll be great. We can talk."

I hesitated. I felt devastated. I thought I was going to be able to pull it off. I had actually come back to work and was functioning.

"I'm coming right now," Maryanne said firmly.

I sighed. "OK," I replied weakly, "I'll be ready."

No one said anything as we left. I was totally autonomous at work. I liked the freedom. Later I called and explained about a mild relapse and that I would continue to keep my appointments and stay in touch.

I tried to relax as Maryanne guided her vintage Mercedes, spoils of her first marriage, onto the freeway. The tremors subsided somewhat. "I have to go back to work for the afternoon, but I'll be home for dinner," Maryanne said over the hum of the Mercedes. "Anyway, I called Robbie and he is really looking forward to taking care of you. He says he understands what you are going through, he's been there. He has a lot he wants to share."

I had for some time intuitively felt that this huge and huge-hearted man who was Maryanne's husband had gifts and knowledge for me. Arriving, I walked through her perfect suburban front door into the massive arms of Rob Wentz. Maryanne left shortly to return to work.

Rob Wentz was six foot four and weighed well over two hundred pounds. A former triathlete, aging and illness had softened his body, but his presence was still larger than life. He had black, wavy hair, huge soft brown eyes, full lips, and warm brown skin. He was often asked if he had Hawaiian ancestors. He was probably the most dynamic, responsive human being I have ever known. He was also extremely intelligent, but it was his emotional side that was so magnetic.

145

Oddly, his intensity was similar to that of my friend, Patty, who had also been labeled manic-depressive. When I compared these two people to others in my life, it seemed to me that they were simply so attuned to their deepest feelings that they were sometimes overcome by them. Perhaps that is why these people often ultimately either commit suicide or become shamans and priests. I wondered if perhaps they were just a more spiritually developed version of each one of us, too highly developed for us to relate to them on normal levels.

Rob Wentz acted as counselor, nurse, father, and spiritual guide for me all that afternoon. He tucked me into his favorite chair, covering me with a soft Afghan, and he opened his heart and Soul to me in a way that impacted me like no one ever had.

He shared his personal story. Born with a cleft palate, one of his first experiences as an infant was to be physically traumatized by the surgery required to correct it. All of his life, he suffered rejection for it. As a child, he was sexually abused by a trusted adult and physically abused by a nun in Catholic school.

He read to me from many of his favorite books. We howled with laughter, we sobbed with grief, and we became one being in a passionate outpouring and exchange of selfless love. In a warm, sunlit room filled with Maryanne's collection of antique teddy bears and her blooming African violets, and with a cat on each of our laps, we journeyed to the very core of our Souls with one another. And the man who had once studied for the priesthood taught me about God—the real, loving, glorious power of God.

When Maryanne arrived home that evening, the three of us enjoyed an intimate dinner together, and then we all shared some more. My body had stilled, but I was beginning to experience wave after wave of the mysterious euphoria that frightened me almost as much as the electrical impulses.

146

I continued for a long, long time to suspect that all of these paranormal experiences I was having, whether physical, mental, or emotional, were crazy. I always knew in my deepest self that they were spiritual, that they were good, and that they would somehow change me irretrievably in a powerfully positive way. Yet, paradoxically ignorant out of my own strong-mindedness, I fought it every step of the way.

Maryanne was as loving and caring as her husband. "You can sleep in Jason's bed," she said. Her voice was warm and soft. Her son, Jason, had continued to be one of Erik's best friends. Jason was currently living with his dad. She helped me into a soft flannel gown, and I sank back into the warm, sloshing waterbed. I felt more relaxed than I had in days. She covered me with a pale gray down comforter. I called that bed the Silver Cloud ever after that.

As I lay in the Silver Cloud waiting for my Xanax to kick in for the night, Rob came to the doorway. "I didn't read this to you today. I didn't know if you were ready, but I've been sitting out there thinking about it and I want to give it to you—not just to read, but like a gift." He handed me a book with a deep blue, heavy paper cover. I read the title that was printed on it in gold: *A Course in Miracles*.

"I've heard about this book," I murmured. "Sandy is reading it. I keep asking her what it's about, but she says she doesn't know how to explain it. I've really wanted to read it. Thank you so much. I'm sleepy. I think I can sleep tonight."

He turned out the light for me and left, closing the door softly.

I woke up at 3 A.M. I was getting used to feeling that I was in another world, though I kept hoping I would wake up feeling normal one of these times. I took a pill and tried to relax back into the Silver Cloud. The familiar race of thoughts began shooting through my mind. I felt a cold shiver rush down my legs. Sitting up, I looked around trying to focus my terrors so I could still them.

I considered calling out for Maryanne or Rob. My eye fell on the blue book on my nightstand. I reached for it and settled it on my lap, letting it fall open. I wasn't about to begin at the beginning of such a long book; besides I was too scattered to be that orderly. Forcing my attention to the pages, I read:

> If to love oneself is to heal oneself, those who are sick do not love themselves. Therefore, they are asking for the love that would heal them, but which they are denying to themselves. If they knew the truth about themselves, they could not be sick.

I felt a strange little thrill run through me. I felt like I had been shocked, but just enough for it to be very, very pleasant. What kind of book was this? As I stared at the lines I had just read, they suddenly seemed to become emblazoned with light. The words echoed in my mind, seeming wiser and more profound than anything I'd ever

147

heard or read. I was convinced at that moment that no ordinary human mind could possibly expound such simple, pure Truth.

And moreover, if it was Truth, it was saying that I had the power to heal my own sickness, and that it had to do with loving myself. I was exhilarated and frustrated at the same time. I knew it was the key, but I didn't know how to love myself.

Well, maybe I should begin at the beginning, I thought. For what seemed like hours, I rocked gently in the warm, sloshing Silver Cloud and became lost in the glorious message of *A Course in Miracles*. Every line of type in this profound book was on fire for me—not only in my mind but also to my physical eyes. It was as though every word had a light behind it. I was reminded of the strange glow of the rose window. Would everything ever stop being so weird? I read other passages:

148

> God has kept your kingdom for you, but He cannot share His joy with you until you know it with your whole mind.
>
> (4.VII.7)

> The escape from darkness involves two stages: First, the recognition that darkness cannot hide. This step usually entails fear. Second, the recognition that there is nothing you want to hide even if you could. This step brings escape from fear. When you have become willing to hide nothing, you will not only be willing to enter into communion but will also understand peace and joy.
>
> (1.IV.1)

Could this have anything to do with the peace I had felt in the deep sharing time with Rob all afternoon?

I realized that the Truth about myself was contained in this book. I had become quite a feminist, but even so, the male-oriented language did not bother me. I knew it was written to accommodate contemporary culture, and I knew it transcended anything as petty as sexism. The words were not the meaning, though the meaning was contained in the words.

I experienced the first real peace since kneeling at the rose window. I slept. I awoke at 7 A.M. I was lying on my back. I still felt calm and relaxed, though once again euphoric and otherworldly. I noticed beams of sunlight streaming across my face from the window behind my head.

Arching my neck, I looked up through the window into the blue, blue morning sky. Centered perfectly in the rectangle of blue and extending beyond the lower and upper frame of the window, splitting it in two, were two absolutely vertical jet trails, one crystal clear, the other wispy, as though the plane had fallen straight down, then turned abruptly and shot straight up.

I felt the warmth rush through me. The obvious, synchronistic meaning of this brilliant cerulean tableau transfixed me. I must emphasize how foreign all this was to my usual practical consciousness. It was clear to me that these jet trails were symbols of what I had experienced that night. For it was the night I really let go of my tight grip on the earthbound world of man's reality and turned toward heaven, allowing myself to begin to believe, really deeply believe, in God.

Time after time in my life, after that morning, when I was struggling with some difficult issue, or elated over some spiritual lesson I had learned, I would look up into the sky and see a white jet trail extending upwards like some mystical guiding sign. I never ceased to be astounded by this synchronicity, but eventually I began to simply accept it as a natural part of my new Spiritual Life.

149

∞

I was uncomfortable as usual to feel tears running down my face, but what I continued to realize was that each time I came out of a memory back to my hospital bed, the tears represented more joy and less pain.

Just then, Dr. Tanner poked her head in my open door and knocked softly on the doorjamb. "Susan, are you awake? May I come in?"

"Sure," I said, sitting up. I fluffed my hair and grabbed a Kleenex to wipe my eyes.

She did not sit. She stood several feet from my bed holding the clipboard in her hands. "We find that you have improved greatly since the day you came in here," she began.

If you only knew, I thought.

"We have decided to release you today. There is a lot of paperwork to do, arrangements to be made. We will need you to stay until later this afternoon. You can call someone and have them come by about four o'clock. And we're referring you to two weeks of day treatment at another hospital. I will also refer you to an outside psychiatrist for a follow-up visit."

I digested this information. It felt comforting to me to think I would have more of this kind of peaceful time. I had benefited from it. "Could I make a request about the psychiatrist?" I asked. "Could it be someone who has a spiritual orientation?"

She looked thoughtful. I thought her voice was just a teensy bit softer as she answered, "I think I know just the one," she said. "His name is Jerry Young. I think you'll like him."

I thanked her. Hesitating, I called out to her as she started to leave, "Dr. Tanner."

She turned and looked at me with those raised eyebrows. "Yes?"

"I just want to thank you." She continued to look surprised. "I learned a lot about myself here. It has turned out to be a very good thing. I have found God on this psych ward."

She looked at me for several moments. Then she nodded and left.

# FIFTEEN

# SAINT BERNADETTE

*. . . the last thing that can help the non-right-minded, or the sick, is an increase in fear. They are already in a fear-weakened state. If they are prematurely exposed to a miracle, they may be precipitated into panic.*

—A COURSE IN MIRACLES (2.IV.4:7–9)

Tuesday, April 18, 1989—Lunchtime: "You walk with Jesus, don't you?"

I stared across the little eating room full of patients at the woman, also a patient, who spoke these words. I had just walked to my table and was about to place my tray on it. The woman, a black woman of about thirty, was standing also. Everyone else in the room was seated.

I was dumbfounded. How did she know this? Why was she saying it to me? Why did she single me out? No one had ever said anything like that to me. I wore no religious symbols, did not practice any obvious rituals. How could she know this?

I had made no progress in relating to the other patients on the ward. I still ate every meal alone, in silence. In spite of the woman's approach, this meal was no exception, though she continued to stare at me all through lunch.

After lunch, I pretended to take a slow walk through the corridors. Inter-patient visiting was prohibited, but I felt I had to talk to the black woman. I finally found her room. She was sitting on her bed with her arms around herself. I glanced around to see that no one was looking, then slipped in and sat on the adjacent bed facing her.

"Why did you ask me if I walked with Jesus?" I whispered.

She looked at me sadly, "I've tried and tried to find him," she said. "I just can't seem to find him. Can you help?"

I reached over and took her hand, another forbidden act. "Would you like to pray with me?" At first, I felt awkward and shy. But as I looked into her eyes, I seemed to find strength there.

"Please," she murmured.

I closed my eyes and spoke a short prayer. When I was finished, I opened my eyes and looked at her. Tears were flowing down her cheeks. I felt a flood of love and compassion for her. I wanted to ask her about her illness, but I was afraid to stay longer. The nurses patrolled regularly.

154

I returned to my room and lay down on the bed. Who was this Jesus, really? I wondered. I had been raised in a basically Christian culture, but I had never gained any real knowledge of this man or his life. All I knew was that his essence, and the traditional symbols and rituals of the religion which bore his name, had been a vital part of my Spiritual Journey of the last four years.

The Christian experience had been a big part of the next stage, the final days of my spiritual awakening before I entered the hospital. These last days were the most frightening, bizarre, and exhilarating yet, and they culminated in the complete breakdown of my endurance and courage.

∞

I had only stayed with Maryanne and Rob one more day during that first week in April when I was introduced to A Course in Miracles and the jet trails. I had then returned home for the weekend, which I had planned to spend with my children. I was still using Xanax. I read my Course in

*Miracles* whenever I felt really terrified. It always soothed and comforted me. Often, though, it also triggered euphoria for me, which brought up more fear because I continued to think that it might just all be part of some mental breakdown.

Oddly, my boyfriend, Jack, who was rather surprisingly still around, had continued to become more accepting of my deteriorating condition as my flu-like symptoms had decreased, and as it had generally become less physical and more mental. He had seemed able to deal with anything as long as we could have sex.

During this mystical Second Episode, sex had turned out to be a powerful trigger for me for intense, spiritually oriented phenomena. I had frequently felt as though I were not in my body. Sometimes I had felt incomprehensibly intense caring for Jack as we made love. He had seemed almost beyond human to me at times, as if he were not Jack but another being, or all beings. And, oddly, I sometimes wouldn't have any memory of the lovemaking in the morning. He would describe the intensity of it with great delight and appreciation and I would just stare at him blankly, as though he must be talking about someone else.

Sometimes I wondered if these experiences were caused by a delayed reaction to my old drinking and drug habits, but I knew these had been relatively mild, even at their peak. Besides, I hadn't smoked any marijuana for many months and I had stopped drinking any alcohol with the onset of my flu.

On Saturday night, I stayed overnight with Jack. I woke up at 3 A.M. or so, as I frequently did. Jack snored softly beside me. At first, I felt loving and euphoric. Then the usual fear gripped my mind. Next, an unusually severe bout of seizures began shaking my body and paralyzing my legs.

All of a sudden, I felt overwhelmed in a burst of utter despair and frustration. I knew I had reached the very

155

bottom, the absolute limit, of my human endurance. I couldn't go on like this any longer. In spite of my new spiritual ideas, I had continued to resist actually calling on a power other than my own, yet I now found myself saying aloud, softly, but with all the intensity of my desperately screaming Soul, "IF THERE IS A GOD, PLEASE, PLEASE HELP ME!"

After a few moments, I began to feel as though I had been suddenly released from a giant vise. My entire body relaxed. I felt formless, almost liquid or gelatinous. At the same time, I seemed to become as light as a feather and almost transparent.

Then came the Light. It was Light so intense that "Light" is not a bright enough name for it. It seemed to fill me—and fill me so fully that it shone out all over me. The mysterious warmth also became part of it. I just let myself be in that radiant Light. I felt waves of rapture throughout my mind and body, and I wanted it to last forever.

156

Then suddenly, but gently, there were Words with the Light. I didn't hear them; they weren't spoken by a voice. I didn't see them; they weren't a vision. They were just in my mind—resembling a thought, but not a normal thought.

The Words were clear and emphatic. Each one seemed a complete expression of pure Love breathed by some ancient, Wise Energy. They were unrelated to anything in my conscious mind, as though someone else put them there instead of my thinking them. The Words were: "*Find out about Saint Bernadette.*"

It seemed like many rapturous hours later that I slowly returned to the relative reality of Jack's bed, still feeling warm, peaceful, and utterly relaxed. I fell into dreamless sleep, but somehow the Words were still there.

The next morning when I woke up, the Words were still there. I felt an odd compulsion to do as the Words instructed. The message didn't say, Saint Bernadette is here for you so everything is fine; it said, find out about her. I told Jack about my experience. He was raised Catholic so I figured he must know about saints.

"Don't know much about her." Jack answered my question as if it were perfectly normal. By this time, I was pretty worried that my behavior was seeming totally crazy. I figured that other people probably thought so, too. It made sense, then, that they would feel like they should be calm and pretend everything I did and said was normal. The odd thing about the craziness was that my deep, intuitive knowing assured me that I was a totally sane person having a spiritual experience. If just one other person had confirmed that authoritatively, it would have alleviated my fear considerably.

On Monday, I still was scheduled to meet at one o'clock with the woman I had called the previous week, the one who had been working on the Jesuit auction, Judy Guardino. I had not gone in to work, but I felt that I could handle an appointment. Moreover, I felt some strange compulsion to meet this woman.

I had not found out anything about Saint Bernadette. One of my friends remembered the old Andy Williams song about Lourdes, the village of Saint Bernadette. That was about the extent of it.

As I drove out to where Judy Guardino lived in an upscale suburban neighborhood with her dentist husband and five children, I kept thinking, I'm supposed to ask Judy Guardino about Saint Bernadette. Remembering that she had mentioned her working on the Jesuit auction when I called, I thought she must be Catholic.

I was mortified at this latest bout of what I considered to be irrationality. How could I show up at the home of a client I had never met, present myself as a professional architectural designer, then ask her about Saint Bernadette because I felt that I was supposed to? Right. Yet I kept feeling certain that I must do this. It made no sense; everything should make sense.

Judy Guardino opened her front door. I smiled at a pleasant, intelligent looking woman about my own age. "Come in," she said. Her voice was warm and friendly. "I can't believe it, but we have the house to ourselves. There's always so much going on with five teenagers, but they're all gone this afternoon so we can have a good talk, uninterrupted." Was I imagining that she was looking straight into my eyes with an unusual intensity?

We walked up a half-flight of stairs into a kitchen with the usual seventies features: There were dark brown stained cabinets with a Spanish design routed into the doors; orange countertops; and a green linoleum floor, also with Spanish motif. Automatically, I mentally cut a skylight into the ceiling and replaced the peninsula with an island. I could picture the new hardwood floors, white laminate Euro-style cabinets, ceramic tile countertop and splash, under-cab lighting, and bright new appliances.

158

"I have lots of ideas already," I told Judy as we both sat down in the old-fashioned nook.

I looked at the woman sitting across from me. She was tall. She had soft, blondish, curly hair and hazel eyes. There was a compelling quality of kindliness and assurance in her face. Trying not to stare, I suddenly perceived a faintly glowing light that seemed to emanate from all around her. At first I thought she was sitting in front of a window I hadn't noticed, but there was no window.

I spoke tentatively, though I was usually very confident on business calls. I did not really want to discuss Judy's kitchen right then, and I knew what I was about to say was not what she expected. "Um . . . I know this probably sounds a little odd, but I've been going through some really mysterious stuff for the last few weeks." I told her all about my illness, then about the awful tremors in my body, the rose window, all my terror and euphoria. I told her everything. Lastly, I told her about the Words that had come to me Saturday night.

"I know this sounds crazy," I whispered. I hesitated, then blurted, "But do you know anything about Saint Bernadette?"

She just looked at me for a long, long moment.

Oh God, now I've done it, I groaned inwardly. She probably thinks I'm nuts, not to mention more than a little unprofessional.

Then I noticed she was smiling a soft, Mona Lisa smile. She reached across the table and took my hands in hers. I felt the warmth of her smile in her hands.

"My dear, I'm so glad you've come to me. I've been praying and fasting for two weeks. God told me someone was coming to me in great distress, someone who needed comfort and counsel. Not only do I know about Saint Bernadette, but I've just recently been to Lourdes, the town in France where she saw her visions of Our Lady and discovered the spring that has healed thousands. I have some holy water from there. I'll give you some when you leave, but now, would you like to pray with me and ask Jesus into your heart?"

The room spun in front of my eyes, then seemed to fill with the familiar Light. I couldn't believe what I had just heard. I couldn't believe this was happening. I was petrified with fear, but it sounded so wonderful. And no one would know—no one else was there.

I prayed and talked with Judy for four hours. We actually got down on our knees and asked together for Jesus to come into my heart. She gave me a little plastic film canister of holy water from Lourdes when I left.

No one will ever believe this, I thought as I drove home. How will I ever tell this to anyone? They will really think I am nuts now. I was astounded by my children's acceptance when I offered to bless them with the holy water. I was awkward at it, devising my own little ritual of making a wet cross on their foreheads and repeating a prayer.

I had shyly asked Jack to teach me a Catholic prayer. He taught me "Hail Mary," struggling to remember it at first, then struggling not to cry as he did. I thought it was beautiful.

My children were obviously mystified by my behavior, and they were agonized when I was distressed, but they seemed enchanted by the loving, spiritual energy I conveyed when I was feeling euphoric. I continued to vacillate between Heaven and Hell for another week. I wouldn't have thought it possible, but both the terror and the euphoria increased. I was again sleeping very little, which contributed to my extremely agitated state.

Continuing to feel a compulsion to connect with people, I spent hours on the phone with friends and relatives I had not talked to in years, expressing effusive love to them all. Surprisingly, they didn't seem to think this inappropriate but actually responded with delight and warmth, sometimes moved to tears. I sent flowers to Boston for my sister, who had not talked to anyone in our family for many months, on her birthday, April 5.

160

Dr. Bob Doughton, a physician turned therapist who was also a dear friend, had begun to treat me during this time. He had continued to prescribe low dosage Xanax for me and had encouraged me to come in for an all-day rebirthing and therapy session. At this time, I did the all-day intensive with him and his insightful, gentle wife, Caroline.

They were loving and patient, trying desperately to understand and help me. They served a lovely lunch for me and shared with me a video about the writing of *A Course in Miracles*. They absolutely believed I was having a profound spiritual experience, but they were perplexed by the intensity of my anxiety and unable to calm my fears.

I finished the day feeling loved but more anxious than ever because the Doughtons had no professional diagnosis to offer. Bob drove me home, afraid to let me drive. He had written me a prescription for a teddy bear, and he stopped at the store on the way home to buy it for me. I bought a Bible at the same time.

Later that weekend, Jack and I drove south to visit my father and my stepmother, Ethel, a nurse. I was in an extreme state of spiritual euphoria that day. I could barely relate to anyone normally. The sky seemed ultra intensely bright and all objects seemed to be filled with shimmering Light. Jack and my father and Ethel all seemed unearthly, angelic.

I didn't feel much like communicating at all. I was aware that I must have seemed withdrawn and deranged to them, but I couldn't explain to them what I was feeling. I went out into my father's backyard and lay on a chaise longue just gazing at the sky. Everything looked so beautiful—so bright and incredible. I didn't want to relate to the real world.

My father was horrified. He and Ethel and Jack all discussed my condition with grave concern. Later, after we had left, they called Dr. Ryan, knowing she had been called once early in my episode. All they knew about Dr. Doughton was that he was giving me medication. In their fear and confusion, they assumed he was perhaps incompetent and was giving me too many drugs, which could be the cause of my extreme state. Because I was exhausted and could not communicate, they also assumed I was depressed and suicidal.

Jack drove me home that night and left me reluctantly. He was beside himself with desperate fear and consternation.

This was the night of April 12.

I went into the house and went to bed, still feeling detached from reality. The euphoria was lessening again, however, and I began to be afraid once more that I was losing my grip. I had no context for defining any of these states of mind or body as positive or holy. My energy was running out. It was so low that I thought life was about to leave me forever. I could not sleep, could not still my mind.

Suddenly, I was overwhelmed with absolute mental and physical exhaustion and hopelessness. I could think of nothing else to do in my own environment. I had reached the end of my personal resources.

Dr. Doughton had warned me not to go to a hospital. "You don't want to end up on some psych ward," he had said emphatically to me. "They will not see anything spiritual about your experience, believe me." But I had no idea where else to turn at that point.

I picked up the phone and called Dr. Ryan. "I think I am dying, Dr. Ryan. I guess I need to go to a hospital," I told her in an exhausted whisper. I had no idea my father had already called her.

"I'll make arrangements," she said. I could tell she was trying to sound professional, but her voice was cautious, almost fearful. "Someone will be there soon. Can you hold on for a couple of hours?"

162

My voice remained weak, but I felt a little less scared already. "Oh yes," I responded, "I've been holding on for days."

∞

I glanced nervously around my hospital room. I actually felt a little anxious thinking about that night when it had all overwhelmed me completely, and I had finally gone over the edge.

I wondered if I was ready to leave the sanctuary of the hospital and return to the real world. I had learned a lot about myself here. I felt that I had discovered a lot of reasons for my ending up here. I knew that I was strengthening my belief in God every day, that this was a new resource for me that would never leave me. Yet I was still afraid. I was still uncertain whether all this newfound peace and strength would last when I got out of here.

# SIXTEEN

# OVER THE EDGE

*The self is in the dark because it is blinded by a light greater than it can bear.*

—SAINT JOHN OF THE CROSS

Tuesday, April 18, 1989—Midafternoon: I was very surprised to see Dr. Ryan walk into my room. I had packed up my few things and was sitting on my bed writing in my journal when she arrived.

"Hello, Susan. I hear you're leaving here this afternoon. I just stopped by to see how you are."

I looked at her. She seemed warm, friendly, concerned. I sensed that she really cared about me. I was glad to see that my feelings of betrayal had lessened considerably in several days of contemplation.

"Hi, Dr. Ryan. I'm much better, thank you. This turned out to be a good rest for me. I guess I needed that." I did not say any more. It seemed pointless to try to explain to her about my spiritual realizations.

She smiled. "Well, call me anytime," she said, "anytime day or night. I'll be there if you need me."

I felt tears coming. "Dr. Ryan," I began, feeling suddenly shy, "could I give you a hug?"

She hesitated for only a second, then hugged me. Her hug felt a little awkward, but sincere.

"I need that from all my doctors," I told her. I was smiling back at her now.

She looked pleased with herself and somewhat thoughtful as she turned and left.

I lay back on my bed to ponder one last time. My mind became filled with thoughts about the climactic night, less than a week ago, when I had called Dr. Ryan to tell her that I felt as though I could not go on. It was the following morning that she had brought me here.

At the time, it had felt like my darkest hour. I was certain that the beautiful, elusive Light that I had kept finding, then losing again, had finally gone out for good. Now I could see that it had simply been the final night before the dawn when I was to awake to this Light and to allow it to fill my life fully, once and for all.

I wondered if Dr. Ryan had been surprised when she visited today to find that I had recovered so quickly. When I came here nearly a week ago, I had been in such a weakened state that I had believed I was near death, and I think she had thought so, too. Closing my eyes, I remembered it clearly. It was just last Thursday morning, April 13, very early:

164

∞

I shivered and huddled further into the corner of the soft, gray flannel couch. I was alone in the living room of my apartment. Outside, the predawn April morning was dark and misty. So was the inside of my head.

I had felt good about my living here. I loved the spacious Victorian rooms. The floor was carpeted in thick, green velvet. The graceful bay window with the stained glass rose section angled toward the street. I thought about how this window, glowing with holy luminescence, had become a compelling focal point for me in recent days. I glanced up at it now, but it appeared dim and lifeless.

I focused on the charming little marble fireplace on the wall opposite the couch. Libbi, now seventeen, lived here with me. Her true vocation, like mine, was art, and I had framed one of her brightly hued abstracts and hung it above the mantle. I thought with satisfaction how her fresh, free-spirited work sold at the gallery much faster than my more polished pieces.

I was waiting for Dr. Barbara Ryan, who had been my regular doctor for four years, to come and take me to the hospital. I was hoping someone there could finally figure out what the hell was wrong with me.

I thought about my past month of crippling physical and psychological symptoms—such as a high fever, severe insomnia, and a distorted sense of reality—which no one had been able to explain or treat effectively. I was beginning to refer to this extraordinary month as my Second Episode because it so resembled the First Episode of four years ago. But the First Episode had been far less severe and had lasted only three days.

I thought about this Second Episode and the many mysterious spiritual phenomena that had been part of it, such as the glowing window and the Saint Bernadette message that had led me to Judy Guardino. Most people, especially the professionals from whom I had sought help, had discounted and trivialized, or simply ignored, these spiritual occurrences.

I was at the absolute end of my strength. My family and friends were depleted, mystified, and frightened. Doctors and therapists were vague and perplexed.

I slowly got up and shuffled into the bathroom. I settled heavily onto the edge of the antique claw-foot bathtub, its cool hardness feeling somehow comforting. Pushing the red cedar door shut, I regarded myself in the full length mirror attached to it. My prematurely white hair hung in damp strands. There were puffy purple crescents underscoring my eyes. Focusing into the black depths of my pupils, I felt the deep panic and confusion that I saw reflected there.

Concurrently, some totally different aspect of me felt compassion and loving concern for this forlorn image.

I realized this was yet another example of the strange duality that had seemed to possess me in a tortuous, endless battle for my sanity. The usual questions haunted my exhausted mind: How much more can I endure? How long will people be willing to help me? Why can't someone tell me what is happening to me? Am I dying, or going mad? How can such a debilitating experience be exhilarating and spiritual at the same time?

I had called Dr. Ryan in the middle of the night and told her I guessed I had better go to the hospital. I had no idea what to expect there, but I just didn't know what else to do. I instinctively knew I had to go somewhere where I could be free of the normal demands of life. I longed to rest completely and surrender to whatever power was attempting to possess me. I felt certain that it would transform me into a new being of Love and Light, if I could just stop fighting it.

166

I basically trusted Dr. Ryan and had assumed she would help me. When I had called her several hours ago, I was surprised that she had readily agreed that the hospital seemed the right place for me to go, and even more surprised when she had offered to come and take me herself. Much later, when I learned that my father had called her earlier that same night, concerned that I was drugged and suicidal, I realized that my expressions of desperation, depletion, and total frustration must have reinforced her concern about this.

I was exhausted and utterly defeated by a process that I couldn't understand, but I wanted only to stop it, to feel all right again. I certainly didn't want to die! What I really wanted was for someone to explain and guide me to the elusive Spiritual Kingdom that I kept glimpsing and disbelieving. I was looking for a way to destroy the dark energy that seemed to pull me away from a glorious, beckoning Light.

Drawing myself up from the rim of the tub, I returned to my post in the living room. A faint gray light was just beginning to illuminate the forms around me. The dark, chilling terror and uncertainty, which had become so familiar to me in the last few weeks, engulfed me once again.

Even when my experiences had made me spiritually euphoric, I was so terrified that this was just a symptom of the onset of some mental disease that I usually found it difficult to accept and believe in them. Some of them, however, had been so overwhelmingly positive and beatific that for a time I forgot to be afraid and simply flowed into the enchantment and glory, as though it was the most natural thing in the world.

But always the fear returned.

I heard a light tap on the front door. Through its oval glass window, I could see the face of Dr. Ryan. My first impression was that she looked a little tired and scared herself in the gloomy light. About my own age of forty-four, she had a kind, gentle, longish face with warm brown eyes and rather broad features. Her body was generous but firm. Her hair dipped in multiple, still deep brown curves around her face. I remembered that she, like myself, was the mother of four children.

167

I intuitively trusted her loving motive to care for me, but just as intuitively knew she had been given no training in medical school for what was happening to me. Still, there was no one else left to turn to.

I opened the door and just looked at her, feeling awkward and weak. I found it very strange to see her standing there on my front porch. I did not know what to say.

She smiled. "Hi. May I come in?" Her voice was soft, tentative.

"Sure," I murmured. I stepped back and held the door open.

We sat facing each other on the couch. "How are you?" she asked. She sounded more friendly than doctorly.

"I don't know."

"Are you ready to go?"

"I guess so," I nodded.

Having no idea how long I would be at the hospital, I planned to take only my purse. I was wearing an outfit I had bought recently: cotton pants and a short-sleeved top—loose, light and comfortable—with pretty peach roses on a navy blue background.

Dr. Ryan rose and stepped toward the door.

"Just a second," I whispered. "I'll be right there."

I went to the door of Libbi's bedroom and opened it a crack. I heard her soft snores. I stepped in and tiptoed over to her bed. This large room also had a high ceiling and green carpet. I looked down at Libbi's face—innocent, peaceful, and half covered with silky, honey-colored hair. My throat tightened with pain at the confusion and upset I had caused her in the last few weeks.

168

There had been times when she was the only one around to help me in my panic and terror. It must have been overwhelming for her at times. I had realized that it was too much responsibility for a seventeen-year-old, but I had not known what else to do.

I shook her and she grumbled in response, "What, Mom?"

"I'm going to the hospital, Honey."

"What?" She woke up a little more.

"I just need to figure out once and for all what is really wrong with me," I said as reassuringly as I could. "Maybe I need to stay and rest for a little while or something. I'll call you and let you know what's going on. I just can't burden you and everybody else anymore. Please call your sister and brothers and tell them I will be fine. I know this is the right thing to do."

"OK, Mom." She was up on one elbow now. "Will you be all right?"

I leaned down and hugged her. I noticed that at seventeen she still smelled like a baby, waking warm and pungent.

"I'll be fine. I think this is the best thing."

"Yeah, maybe you're right." She seemed to relax as she really let in what I was saying. "Call me. I love you."

"I love you, too," I whispered.

I walked back through the apartment, brightening softly now in the growing morning glow. Taking a last look around, I sighed, not knowing when I would be back here.

Dr. Ryan and I descended the hundred-year-old wooden steps to the street. Narrow and quaint, it was usually bustling with people and traffic, but now it, like Libbi, lay still asleep in the gray mist of early dawn.

Hesitating, I suddenly exclaimed, "Could you wait just a second? I forgot something."

"Take your time," she responded.

I went back into the house and picked up my new Bible and my copy of *A Course in Miracles*. Since Rob Wentz had given me the book, I had learned that it was fast becoming the main source of spiritual guidance for hundreds of thousands of people. I had never read religious books before but had become deeply attached to these two in the last few weeks, finding that they said the same things in different ways. I felt comforted and strengthened carrying them under my arm.

So, not speaking, Dr. Ryan navigated her little car through the equally silent streets, heading for the hospital. We crossed the river into the northeast section of the city.

As we got closer to the hospital, I realized that I really didn't know what to expect. I continued to feel that I had to find someone to take care of me, to understand. The only place I could think of where adults were taken care of was a hospital. I had no expectations beyond that, no pictures of what form this care would take.

It seemed odd to be in a car instead of an examining room with Dr. Ryan. As we drove into the parking lot, I looked up to see an imposing tower topped by a large cross silhouetted black against the glowing morning sky. I saw it as a welcome sign, and I was warmed with wonder at the power that was being generated by these heretofore meaningless symbols in my life.

As we walked through the gleaming, silent corridors of the hospital, a soft voice began speaking a morning prayer over the loudspeaker. It all fit perfectly, and I felt as though I had come home to a place of comfort and help. I felt relieved, relaxed, and peaceful.

We entered a suite of offices, and I sat in the waiting room, as Dr. Ryan said she needed to do some paperwork. After about twenty minutes, she returned to sit beside me on a couch for the second time that morning. It still felt a little awkward.

She had me sign some papers. I did not read them. "Just a formality," she assured me. "I've referred you to Dr. Laura Tanner." She spoke calmly and earnestly. "I think you'll really like her. She's very nice and understanding—and very good. She's actually a friend of mine."

"Thank you," I responded gratefully.

"OK," she said, standing, "follow me and we'll get you settled."

I rose and followed her, feeling more blissful by the moment. We approached a pair of double doors with wire reinforced windows in them. I couldn't wait to crawl into a clean-smelling bed, assisted and soothed by a kindly nurse, and just close my weary eyes and drift into long, long sleep. It sounded heavenly. The doors were opened for us by a green-clad attendant who did not look kindly to me. A few moments later, I heard the click that filled my heart with terror. My first thought was, why didn't I listen to Dr. Doughton?! I had no idea that I was about to begin my six-day Journey to the Light on the lockup ward.

∞

I looked around the green room that had been home for nearly a week. The late afternoon sun made the usual patterns on the walls. I realized that it had been sunny every day that I had been here. How I longed to feel the sun on my skin.

I had completely forgiven Dr. Ryan for bringing me here. I knew now that she had been confused. I also knew how persuasive and demanding my father, who believed I was suicidal at the time, could be. We had all been scared to death. Yet everything had turned out fine. I was well on my way to Spiritual Healing. Once again, I could see that there was Divine Purpose in absolutely everything.

I got up and tucked my journal and my precious holy books into my bag. I also packed the navy blue cotton outfit with the peach roses that I had worn every day here, and that I would forevermore call my Crazy Pajamas. I was ready to go home—back to my children, back to my work, back to my church, back to the real world.

171

# SEVENTEEN

# PARADISO

*When the Mystic Virtue becomes clear, far-reaching,*
*And things revert back to their source,*
*Then and then only emerges the Grand Harmony.*

—LAO-TSE, THE BOOK OF TAO

T uesday, April 18, 1989—4:00 P.M.: I was released
from the hospital. An attendant wearing the name-
tag "Steve" came to my door for me. "Are you ready, Ms.
Brewster?" he asked. His tone still seemed cool but less
unfriendly than it had six days before.

"I sure am," I replied. I walked over to the window and
looked out on the freeway for the last time. I hope we meet
someday, I said silently to the unknown occupants of the
speeding cars.

Once again I was surprised to find tears in my eyes—
this time, as I looked around my room for the last time. I
had done a lot of healing and reinventing of myself in this
room, on this bed, leaning back against these pillows. I was
leaving a lot of my old self here. My tears were not so much
for this loss, however, as they were tears of compassion for
my past suffering, and the suffering of the others here on
this ward, where God was so often longed for and so
rejected.

I gathered my belongings and followed Steve down the
corridor, through the TV viewing room, where I had redis-

covered this relaxing pastime, and out to the locked double doors that I had walked through in such confusion and fear nearly a week before. Jack was waiting to take me home. He took my things. Steve turned the key to unlock the doors, and I heard that same click that had chilled my blood six days before. I walked out the doors, nodding to him without speaking as I left. I had grown to understand the attendants and their difficult jobs much better over my stay, but I still had not felt inclined to get close to them.

Jack and I walked down the long corridors of the hospital, down a flight of stairs, and out into the late afternoon of a perfect spring day. Nothing will ever equal the exhilaration I felt at the moment I crossed that threshold, out into the free fresh air. I looked all around, very slowly, taking it all in. Everything looked new, but to me it was not just new, it was born again. It was as though it was all being created for the first time, just for me—every bud, every little chartreuse leaf and blade.

174

I couldn't believe the intensity of the smells and the sounds. A dog's bark and a honking horn sounded like Bach to my hungry ears. The sun caressing my body felt like warm, radiant love. We got into the car and drove out of the hospital parking lot. I looked back at the cross, high atop the tower. It was shining in the lowering sun.

As we drove through one of my old neighborhoods, I asked Jack to stop at the park, just a few blocks from the Big House. Almost before the car had stopped at the curb, I jumped out and ran to the grass and fell down hugging the earth, snorting its smells like a wild beast.

"If they could see you now, they'd put you right back in there," Jack said, laughing.

"God, I wish I had the words to tell you how this feels," I told him. "I know this was part of a plan to help me really appreciate life."

"There must be an easier way," he sighed.

Poor Jack. I knew this had been hard on him, too. I looked at him. "No matter what, I will always really appreciate your being here today, right now, doing this," I said to him. I meant it with all my heart.

When I got home, I climbed the worn stairs to the porch of the old green Victorian slowly, savoring every step. I threw open the door.

"Girls, I'm home!" I hollered.

Jaqui and Libbi flew into my arms. "My gosh, girls, the house looks wonderful," I exclaimed. It was obvious they had cleaned and polished everything. They had rearranged the furniture, and there were fresh flowers on the table. Best of all, I smelled a fabulous chicken dinner cooking.

Later, when they were serving dinner, I glanced at the rose window in the living room. It was illuminated only by the setting sun, naturally, but for me it seemed to shine with the renewed hope of this day. I felt extremely happy and grateful—and holy.

175

My two weeks in day treatment at another area hospital for outpatient therapy extended and enriched my learning experience. I took classes like assertiveness training that deepened my self-appreciation and my awareness of my authentic, loving Spiritual Power. I met a lot more wonderful people who were struggling to know themselves—and God.

One day after classes, I visited Judy Guardino—the woman who had taught me about Saint Bernadette—who lived close by. She was impressed and inspired by my Easter week experience. "You know, Susan," she said, "I wonder if you would go and visit my sister-in-law, Joan. She is on the psych ward at your day treatment center. She has been manic-depressive for twenty years. I think maybe you could comfort her."

She told me some of Joan's sad history. She had been in and out of institutions for years. Judy and her husband had cared for her in their home many times. "The disease of manic-depression," Judy told me, "is progressive and incurable, they say. I never give up on anything, but I've become pretty discouraged."

I didn't have any idea how I could be of any help to Joan, but I told Judy I would be happy to go see her. The next afternoon after treatment, I went upstairs to the psych ward to visit her. This was not a locked ward and the atmosphere felt different here than that on the ward where I had been. I was pretty sure it was because these people were not prisoners. By that time, I was feeling a powerful compulsion to connect with Joan. On an impulse, I had brought my teddy bear, the one Dr. Doughton had bought for me, to give to her.

The nurses on the psych ward were delighted to see me. Joan was apparently a favorite of theirs. They had told her only that she had a visitor. She approached me down the long corridor of the ward with obvious anticipation. When she saw that I was a stranger, she hesitated. Joan had been a teacher for many years. Intelligence and sensitivity shone from her eyes, and I immediately felt drawn to her.

"I'm Susan Brewster." I grasped her hands in mine and looked at her face intently. "I know your sister-in-law, Judy." I hesitated a moment, then continued, "I brought you a teddy bear. I don't know if you like teddy bears."

She took the soft, fuzzy creature from me and stroked it. "Can you come into my room for a while?" she asked. She spoke in warm, low tones.

"I'd like that," I responded.

We went into her room. She placed the bear ceremoniously on her bed. "Cute," she murmured. "Thanks."

We made idle chit chat for only ten or fifteen minutes, but I could feel an unspoken bond of love between us. I left feeling frustrated and mystified by the tragedy of the debilitating disease that was altering irretrievably the life of this woman of obvious intelligence and integrity. She seemed so normal.

What was this disease of manic-depression? How could it so affect wonderful people like Joan or Patty or Rob? And how could a society that could send people to the moon allow the lives of such fine people to be so devastated? Why didn't somebody do something? I believed God could do something. Too bad Freud, an atheist, became the guru of psychiatry, I thought, instead of Jung, his one-time partner and a very spiritual man. Not for the first or last time in my life, I wished I had the time for a whole new career—this time as a spiritual psychiatrist.

A week or so after my visit with Joan, at a Wednesday night service at LEC we had a wonderful speaker who talked about *A Course in Miracles*. Afterwards, there was a speaker's reception with coffee and refreshments in the Friendship Room. At this gathering, I struck up a conversation with a pleasant woman who told me she was traveling with the speaker, and that she was a psychiatric nurse.

"I really enjoyed your friend's talk, especially his references to *A Course in Miracles*," I told her. "It is a powerful resource for me."

She smiled into my eyes, then said she felt moved to tell me the following story:

> Once we had a patient on the ward where I worked. All the doctors had declared her hopeless and incurable. She had eaten away most of the skin from both of her arms. I asked the doctors if I could have some time with her. There was nothing to lose, so they consented. I read to her from the *Course in Miracles* every day for a number of weeks. That was all I did. Today she is teaching Sunday school. She is completely well.

This was another of those strange coincidences, I realized. I still wondered sometimes why I was hearing a story

177

or encountering a particular person or experience. I was gaining increasing respect for my intuitive knowing, for the internal messages that now seemed to guide my life. I had learned to notice the little synchronous happenings—and some not so little—that are part of all our lives if we just become aware of them.

After my two weeks of day treatment, I returned to work as a designer. I went for my follow-up visit to Dr. Young, who was very kind and very reassuring. "You will never have a recurrence of what you experienced," he said. I was not sure if he believed something he was not professionally allowed to say about the spiritual nature of my mysterious episode, or if he thought that reassuring me would make me feel more relaxed and confident, less susceptible to another psychotic episode.

Dr. Young also told me he thought I was angry with men. I told him I knew I had a lot of healing to do in that area. He seemed impressed. He told me I need not come back to see him again. He said he would prescribe some Xanax for me, but suggested I taper off it as soon as possible.

By September, five months after my release from the hospital, things had settled pretty much into a comfortable pattern. I had tapered myself off Xanax. I was feeling generally relaxed and confident about work and was starting to make money again. I was still seeing Jack, though I didn't think it would last much longer. We just didn't have enough in common now. I was becoming more involved at LEC, teaching Sunday School and trying to learn more about God and service.

One day in early September, Rob Wentz called me and said he would like to introduce me to a man he had met. The man was in town on business, and Rob was bringing him to church Sunday. He sounded excited. I said I would love to meet his friend. "Maryanne and I will be a little late," he said. "I told this fellow to meet you out front. He is short, but well built, has hair almost as gray as yours, and he has the most astounding eyes you've ever seen. His name is John Anderson." He paused for breath. "There's something about this guy—you're going to like him!"

I did like him.

I told Jack as gently as I could that I had met someone else I wanted to date. He shocked me by sobbing for two hours in my arms, much as Jaqui had once done. I was again amazed at how deeply, and for how long, some of us repress our pain.

For ten days, John and I traveled in his little Luv pick-up truck all over eastern Oregon, visiting my favorite spots on earth. I shared the Painted Hills with him. It is so quiet there, you cannot hear a single sound. We ran, laughing and shrieking, through the Blue Gorge, a magnificent turquoise valley full of fossils. We sang to old tunes on the radio—and we fell in love.

179

John was unlike any other man I had ever known. He was sweet and gentle and very, very spiritual. He had a master's degree in philosophy and, wearing the turban of a Sikh and teaching Kundalini yoga, he had traveled and lived all over the country with a group of hippies in the sixties. His hair was prematurely silver like mine, and Rob was right about his eyes. They were light green, so light as to seem almost luminous. He was three years younger than I and he adored everything about me. My recent experience and hospitalization did not put him off—on the contrary, he seemed fascinated and enchanted by it.

John flew back to Florida and called me to propose on a Saturday night, not quite two weeks after we had met. We had a wonderful wedding on the beach in Florida with all his family and friends, then came back to do it again for mine. We even had two honeymoons.

As it turned out, we had both done The Forum, where we had learned that we need to live out of our commitments, not our feelings. John and I were both committed to our marriage. Feeling loved and secure, I began to sleep soundly through every night with my new husband. The foundation of both our lives was God and Spiritual Practice. We created an altar in our house, something that was new for me and a wonderful constant reminder of the presence of God in my life.

John had been a publisher for a number of years. Together, we decided to produce a line of greeting cards called Cosmic Cat. I did the drawings of the grinning furry feline based on our cat, Bart. Then I researched for hours to find loving, caring, positive quotations by famous people. At first, it was just for fun, but the cards took off and became our main source of income.

I wish I could say our marriage was one hundred per-cent idyllic and God-conscious, but we fought bitterly at times as our deepest old wounds surfaced. The basic differ-ence in this marriage for both of us was our spiritual focus, and it began to help us heal. I found myself addressing a lot of old co-dependent issues. I didn't have to count on John for all my sourcing like I had with Bob in my first marriage; this time I had God.

In 1993, we moved to the southern coast. We estab-lished a community of friends through Unity Church and our lives became full. We did a marriage workshop with Ken Keyes, then led one at our church.

I continued to learn and grow as I dealt with the same old issues and concerns. I struggled with my weight and the constant low self-esteem I had around my body, especially as I aged. I worried about my children as they matured and began to deal with their own addictions and conflicts.

I tried to communicate everything honestly, and I tried to learn to forgive and to come as much as possible from a heart place. I became a hospice volunteer. Learning about death and helping the dying profoundly forwarded my spir-itual education.

I knew that something had irretrievably changed at my very core. I was building my life on a whole new foundation. I had learned the Truth. I had met the Christ within me, the living Christ who sourced my every breath, my every decision, my every action. I was home in the Light, my Spirit and my Soul released to co-create my life with God.

# EIGHTEEN

# ILLUMINATION

*The process of creating a mandala moves one gradually towards the inner area, God realization, the Source, the Light, identifying oneself with each stage as one progresses.*

—DR. CARL JUNG, PSYCHOLOGIST

Spring 1991—Two years after my release from the hospital: I finally began to receive information about the true nature of my traumatic Spiritual Episodes. It started to come to me one afternoon when I was at home working on an art project:

I licked the end of my right middle finger, wiped most of the moisture off on a tissue, and placed it gingerly at the edge of an almost impossibly thin sheet of eighteen karat gold, measuring about two inches by three inches. Picking up the sheet of gold from the top of the pile, I moved it very slowly so that the air wouldn't crumble it to pieces. Positioning it above the upper right-hand corner of my watercolor, I then floated it softly down onto the figure of the moon that was painted there. Pressing it gently against the tacky cement, I waited for several minutes, then burnished it with a soft rag. I leaned the painting against the wall and stood back a few feet to critique it. The moon shone with the rich yellow patina of real gold.

Pleased, I lay down on the bed to rest. I had worked nonstop for two weeks, painting the large watercolor mandala. "Mandala" is a Sanskrit word meaning "circle," and many Eastern cultures have created these ancient, basically circular, spiritually symbolic designs. The gold illumination was a final touch. I had gotten the inspiration for it from some ancient illumined manuscripts I had seen at an abbey, south of the city. I was so happy to be painting again. I didn't know why I was painting the mandala really. It just seemed to want to come out of my Soul. I could see that it symbolized my Spiritual Journey.

While painting it, I had experienced an illuminating insight: I suddenly felt a deep knowing that God had just as much fun putting together the shapes and brilliant colors of all the different flowers of the world as I had while painting the mandala. Moreover, I saw that all processes of creating are done with one great Mind. We are continually co-creating with God, each a segment of this Mind, like a hologram. I had heard this concept before and understood it intellectually, but at this moment I knew that it was Truth on some deep, mystical level.

As I lay there looking at the mandala, noticing its brilliance, its duality and symmetry, I felt myself drawn toward the shining core, toward the Light at the center of it. I felt blissful, centering myself. After a few moments, I returned to rational reality and began to think about my life and how everything in it was so infused with God and the Holy Spirit ever since my transformational experience two years ago. Smiling at the memories and gazing at the mandala, I grew sleepy and slept for an hour or so.

I awoke to a light tap on my door. It was Sandy, stopping by for a visit on her way to a project. She had developed her own business and was now a busy building contractor. She came into the house and gave me a big hug, noticing that I was carrying a paintbrush. "What are you painting?" she asked. She saw the mandala and gasped, staring at it for several minutes. "My God, Sue, that is gorgeous. It mesmerizes me. It's just breathtaking."

"I'm pleased with it," I said. "It really expresses some-thing important to me." I explained some of the symbolism to her. "I had no idea when I was painting it what the figures meant," I told her, "but I have a book on symbology, and they are very meaningful. For example, the tree repre-sents the Tree of Knowledge, the butterfly symbolizes meta-morphosis or rebirth. I think it all represents my Spiritual Journey."

"I can see that," she said softly. "It's stunning." Her voice became more businesslike as she continued, "Listen, I want to hear more about it, but I have an appointment. I can only stay a minute. I stopped by to give you this woman's name. I was talking to a gal from church—you don't know her—and she mentioned someone having something she called a 'spiritual emergency.' It sounded a lot like your experience. She told me about a woman who has studied this and knows a lot about it, so I got her name for you."

I thanked her and hugged her and closed the door behind her thoughtfully. I still hungered for information about my experience of over two years ago. I had taken medication for only a few months after I left the hospital, gradually growing stronger and more peaceful each day. I had never had another symptom, but I still harbored a secret fear that I had simply had a nervous breakdown and that I had imagined all the spiritual stuff to get me through it. What didn't make sense about this explanation was that I was still in that spiritual place. I rarely discussed my Episodes with anyone because I never was sure how they would react—especially to my hospitalization.

All I knew was that I had absolutely been profoundly and unmistakably changed by the events of two years ago. It was quite simple: there was no God in my life, then God was my life.

I decided to call the woman right away. She turned out to be extremely nice and very informative. She told me about an organization of psychiatrists and other mental health care professionals based in California called the Spiritual Emergency Network (SEN). She gave me the names of several books and publications by this group.

Distinguished psychiatrist Stanislav Grof and his wife, Christina, who headed up the SEN, had written some of the best books. Another one that the woman recommended highly was titled, *Helping People in Spiritual Emergency*, written by a psychologist, Dr. Emma Bragdon. She also mentioned books by psychiatrists Roberto Assagioli and R. D. Laing, as well as *The Interior Castle*, by Saint Teresa of Avila. She promised to send me some tapes on Kundalini awakening.

I went to the library the next day and checked out what they had. I also found some other books that sounded interesting and applicable. What wasn't there, I found at the local bookstore. Obviously, I wasn't the only person interested in this topic.

Later that evening, as John and I sat reading together, I opened a book titled *Spiritual Emergency, When Personal Transformation Becomes a Crisis*. It contained essays by a number of well-known psychiatrists and others and had been put together by Stanislav and Christina Grof. I read:

> Feelings of oneness with the universe. Sensations of vibrant currents of energy coursing through the body, accompanied by spasms and violent flashes of brilliant light. Fears of impending insanity, even death.
>
> Anyone experiencing such extreme mental and physical phenomena would instantly be labeled psychotic by most modern Westerners. Yet increasing numbers of people seem to be having unusual experiences similar to those described above, and instead of plunging irrevocably into insanity, they often emerge from these extraordinary states of mind with an increased sense of well-being, and a higher level of functioning in daily life. In many cases, long-standing

emotional, mental, and physical problems are healed
in the process.

I was stunned. I turned to John, pointing to the book.
I tried to speak. My lips moved, but no sound came out.

"Honey, what's the matter?" he asked.

"It's all here. Someone understands. They know what
happened to me. It talks about the shaking, the fear of dying
or going crazy.

"It . . . it . . . everything," I finished lamely, tears of joy
and relief running down my cheeks.

I read steadily for several days. I felt that I was starving
for this information, as though I couldn't get enough, fast
enough. I read about many symptoms and characteristics of
spiritual crises that were identical to mine, such as how the
mind can seem to split, frequently evoking images of a battle between Light and Dark, Good and Evil.

I read about Kundalini energy and Kundalini awakening—an ancient Eastern yogic phenomenon—in an essay
by Dr. Lee Sannella, psychiatrist and ophthalmologist. I was
shocked by how this paralleled my Episodes:

187

> Kundalini is seen as an "energy" that usually resides
> "asleep" at the base of the spine. When this energy is
> "awakened" it rises slowly up the spinal canal to the
> top of the head. This may mark the beginning of a
> process of enlightenment.

I remembered the night I had sat in the bathroom of
the Big House, and the powerful energy had traveled up my
spine to my head.

Dr. Sannella wrote about the difference between
Kundalini awakening and psychosis. I found this particularly fascinating because of my hospitalization:

> Our results indicate a clear distinction between the
> physio-Kundalini complex and psychosis, and pro-

vide a number of criteria for distinguishing between these two states. We have seen . . . that a schizophrenic-like condition can result when the person undergoing the Kundalini experience receives negative feedback, either from social pressure or from the resistances of his own earlier conditioning.

That explains why I and everyone else thought I was mentally ill, I thought. I remembered how terrified I was that I was schizophrenic.

I was elated and relieved to read Dr. Sannella's optimistic analysis of the positive effects of Kundalini awakening:

188

> Our results support the view that this force is positive and creative. Each one of our cases is now successful on his or her own terms. They all report that they handle stress more easily, and are more fulfilled than ever before in relationships with others. But in the initial stages, the stress of the experience itself, coupled with a negative attitude from oneself or others, may be overwhelming and cause severe imbalance.

Where was this doctor when I needed him?!

I also learned from Dr. Sannella's essay that the Kundalini process can last over a period of several years and go through various stages. I believed that my awakening had begun with my First Episode, progressed more gently through the following four years of spiritual lessons and growth, and culminated with my Second Episode that had the characteristics of a full-blown spiritual emergency.

In Dr. Emma Bragdon's book, I read that often a spiritual emergency lasts exactly forty days. I got out my journals from the time of my spiritual emergency two years before, and my calculator. I punched in the date I had become ill, then the date I was released from the hospital. I was almost afraid to look, but then I stared at the number on the little screen: 40.

I read about the misunderstanding and abuse that is common in response to spiritual emergencies by the Western medical establishment. I read about the need for loving, knowledgeable support for this experience as it increases in this society, and how many other cultures respect and revere spiritual episodes identical to mine. In Tibet, for example, an initiate like me would be honored and tenderly relieved of all household responsibilities until he or she had completed the arduous, often terrifying journey to God-realization.

Perhaps the most startling information of all, however, I found in *The Interior Castle*, Saint Teresa of Avila's account of spiritual awakening, where I was astounded to read about communications from God known as "locutions." These are specific phrases or sentences God directs to tortured Souls in the form of mysterious, inexplicable mental messages. Saint Teresa writes:

> There is another way in which the Lord speaks to the soul . . . the locution takes place in such intimate depths and a person with the ears of the soul seems to hear those words from the Lord.

She goes on to explain how such a locution from the Lord differs from ordinary thoughts or imaginary assurances which might be created by a worried mind. Anyone who believes they have received such a message direct from God naturally questions its authenticity:

> Furthermore, if the soul is attentive, it can always have assurance for the following reasons: First, there is a difference because of the clarity of the locution. It is so clear that the soul remembers every syllable. Second, in these locutions one often is not thinking about what is heard (I mean that it comes unexpect-

189

edly), and it often refers to things about the future that never entered the mind, so the imagination couldn't have fabricated it. The words are very different. Together with the words, in a way I wouldn't know how to explain, there is often given much more to understand than is ever dreamed of without the words. A true locution produces peace and light in the soul.

"Find out about Saint Bernadette." The words still rang clearly in my memory. I remembered telling Judy Guardino about the mysterious locution. I remembered how she had not only told me all about the sweet saint who saw visions of Mary, but gave me holy water from Lourdes.

I talked to John about it all. "What I really can't believe is that a society that purports to be advanced and progressive could still be locking people up in mental institutions for this," I told him. "I mean, you and I are college graduates. So are almost all of our friends. We are articulate, educated, and keep up with all the latest developments in the world we know."

John nodded in agreement. "That's true, Honey."

I continued, my frustration mounting, "How could there be such gross ignorance of anything so fundamental to humanity as its spiritual growth, its transformation from the darkness of spiritual ignorance to the glorious Light of God consciousness—and not just ignorance, but abuse? I have to do something, John. I have to help. There have to be people out there, thousands of them, who are still as ignorant as I was. It's like this is still in the realm of some underground movement or something."

"You're right, Dear."

"For God's sake, the whole Eastern world recognizes spiritual transformation," I went on. "Ancient tribes had a healthier sense of spiritual life than our modern culture. I have to do something. I have to start telling my story. Even if only one person who needs help hears it and knows, it will be a service to God and to my beloved fellow humans. I have to tell my story."

"You write it, Susan, and I'll help you publish and market it," my husband promised.

"Thanks for believing in me," I told him. I gave him a big hug and kiss. "And thanks for loving me."

Some months later, I began writing *Divine Intervention*. In the course of my research, I found out something which I had not known during my stay on the psych ward: In her native France, April 16—the momentous Easter Sunday of my week in the hospital—is Saint Bernadette's Feast Day.

# EPILOGUE

*As long as space endures,*
*And for as long as sentient beings remain,*
*Until then, may I too abide,*
*To dispel the misery of the world.*

—SHANTIDEVA

July 1998: As *Divine Intervention* is about to go to the editors and layout people, I am told that this is my last chance to update my story. It has been nearly ten years since the events of my transformational Easter Week.

Have I changed? Emphatically yes—and no.

My real source of comfort and joy comes from following my spiritual path. Though people and nature nurture me and art keeps me sane, I now believe that a living, loving spirit transcends these transient things. I feel lonely, but never alone and I am no longer afraid to die.

The ups and downs of my life continue to confound me. John and I divorced amicably a year ago. I am inevitably drawn into my children's various triumphs and tragedies. I struggle with my aging and imperfect body.

I know that no one is evil, that there is an amoral cause for everything, including violent behavior. Yet I still react when I think that I have been attacked. As soon as I think of it, I ask for spiritual guidance, but compassion and forgiveness come slowly.

I once read something profound in a book written by a Christian missionary. She said that to make her life wonderful, she had only to do one thing: She had to remember to think about God every fifteen minutes. I'm up to about twice a day.

I am deeply moved by the sorrows of the world and I want to fix everything. I find volunteering and serving others to be the most gratifying, fulfilling activity of my life. Yet I use very unsaintly excuses like time and money not to do enough.

I go to church. The rituals make me feel light and hopeful and close to people. However, I choose my religions carefully. I don't believe that God is a person whose sole purpose is to teach me some moral dogma. To me, God is the Creative Power of Love, and organized religion is simply two or more people agreeing to meet and tap into it together.

I wear a silver cross on a silver chain. It is a symbol to me of the Truth of Unconditional Love taught by Jesus. I believe that we are all striving to live this Truth in our lives, no matter how it looks. When we realize this, realize our own eternal goodness, then we are saved. Very simply, that is my version of Christianity.

On the physical side, I try to take better care of myself. I eschew deadlines, early morning appointments, and hurrying. I watch TV and I read fiction. Stuff is not so important to me anymore—relationships and creative expression are everything. I make my living as an artist and writer. I live a spare and simple life and I love it, though I have not yet learned how not to feel defensive about it.

I continue to encounter and be amazed by spiritual synchronicities, much like those that played such a major role in my transformative episode in 1989:

Summer 1995: One night, John and I decided to read *The Divine Comedy*. I was astonished by Dante's account of his journey into the "Inferno," through "Purgatorio," and into "Paradiso." This was a spiritual emergency.

My attention became riveted on a line in the footnotes: "The imaginary date of the poem's beginning is the day before Good Friday in 1300." I got out my old journal. Sure enough, the day I had entered the lockup ward, my own personal inferno, was the day before Good Friday in 1989.

January 1998: I had left John and was living with a psychologist friend. After reading my manuscript of *Divine Intervention*, she said to me, "Since you and John will probably not publish this now, I think you should show it to Cindy Black, a publisher friend of mine."

I made an appointment the next day and drove out to where Beyond Words Publishing, Inc. had just moved into a beautiful new space in a large business complex. It was a clear, sunny day. As I drove along, I saw up ahead the building Cindy had described to me. Two white jet trails emanated from behind it, upward into the blue, blue sky.

God bless you,
Susan Anderson, 1998

195

Special thanks to Sulie, Libbi, Erik, Jaqui, Leigh, Ann, Sandy, Sallyanne, Jim, John, Ruth, Cindy, and Drs. Robert, Karen, Bob, Susan, and David.

# AFTERWORD

## WHAT TO DO IN A SPIRITUAL EMERGENCY

hat do you do if you are in spiritual crisis? How can you help a friend, a family member, or a patient who is disturbed by events related to spiritual experiences? This section provides a quick reference guide for addressing these potentially growthful experiences.

Below is a list of indicators of spiritual emergency and two checklists to follow while managing the crisis. The sequence within each checklist is especially important to follow. Also note that these suggestions are not a substitute for professional help; I advise anyone in crisis to seek appropriate counseling.

Additionally, on page 202 there is a checklist addressed to a health care provider who is needing to diagnose, make a prognosis, and create a treatment program.

To all concerned: People who are experiencing spiritual emergence phenomena are going through a powerful rebirth that opens the heart and spirit. They need compassion for themselves and from others. Everyone involved needs to be respectful—as you would be with someone in the process of physical birth. Things can get messy, loud, tense, exquisitely sensitive, quiet, inspiring, dull, too long, too short, and out of control. Everything seems to work out with the least pain and suffering when everyone goes with the flow—allowing the contraction and expansion inherent in nature—in an environment of peace and safety.

## HOW TO IDENTIFY A SPIRITUAL EMERGENCY:

A spiritual emergency will include some or all of the following:

1. Sudden re-evaluation of religious affiliation and/or beliefs
2. Lack of interest in eating or sleeping due to excited state of inspiration
3. Dramatic symbolic experiences of death and rebirth; may include or be part of near-death experience
4. Mythological and archetypal phenomena
5. Past incarnation memories
6. Out-of-body experiences
7. Synchronicities, premonitions (clairvoyance), or extrasensory perceptions
8. Intense energetic phenomena—e.g., electrical sensations, vibrations, or spasms
9. States of mystical union or identification with cosmic consciousness
10. Visions and/or creative inspiration
11. Mental messages which are clearly beneficent in nature; clairaudience

Anyone in spiritual emergency will be able to perceive his/her experience with a positive, exploratory attitude and be able to maintain a trusting relationship with an appropriate person. If this attitude is not evident, the spiritual crisis may be attended by psychological problems.

## IF YOU ARE IN CRISIS AND BELIEVE
## IT IS A SPIRITUAL EMERGENCY:

1. Consult a physician, nurse practitioner, or other health care professional to rule out physical causes.

198

Thyroid and hormone imbalances, problems with metabolizing sugars, and some allergies are just a few of the physical conditions that can effect strong psychological symptoms.

2. Find a sympathetic, knowledgeable "ally."

This can be a friend, family member, pastoral counselor, psychotherapist, or physician. Someone who has been through a similar experience is ideal. The ally needs to be able to listen with compassion, see the positive aspects of the process, provide a true sense of safety, function as an advocate, and get additional help when and if needed. Most importantly, this person needs to be available for you.

3. Preferably with your ally, verbalize or write the answers to the following questions to determine the parameters of your spiritual emergency:

   a.   Do I have feelings of wanting to hurt myself or die? If these feelings are insistent or overwhelming, contact a physician or crisis center as soon as possible. If the feelings are not overwhelming or insistent, they may be indicative of a symbolic death—as if your innermost being is recognizing that you are shedding your skin in a natural process of growth.

   b.   Am I afraid, anxious, or depressed?

   c.   Am I having trouble getting adequate sleep or food?

   d.   Am I so emotional that I may need medications for a while to help me become more calm and centered?

e. Do I feel estranged from my family, friends, co-workers, or partner?

f. Do I feel a great need for companionship and reassurance?

g. Can I take care of my basic personal needs—food, shelter, money?

h. Can I keep my attention on my personal goals?

i. Do I need a respite from my personal responsibilities? If so, do I know what my options are?

4. With your ally, set up a program to solve these problems and meet these needs. Figure out what is most important to you right now and how you can bring it into your life. You might do some or all of the following processes:

a. Ask your ally to listen to you. Especially if you tend to be spacey, conversing with your ally is usually grounding. Stay connected—don't isolate. Schedule phone calls with supportive friends. Even if your ally is a professional counselor, ask for frequent visits or a daily phone call if you need it. Not feeling isolated may be the difference between a positive and negative experience. Limit your socializing to people who are uplifting or comforting.

b. Take walks. Repetitive, rhythmic physical exercise is helpful—e.g., stretching, easy yoga postures, gardening, swimming, dancing. Being in nature is ideal.

c. Eat in a quiet atmosphere. Avoid alcohol, sugar, caffeine, and stimulants.

d.   Listen to harmonic, peaceful music.

e.   Get nonsexual massage. You want to calm your system. Sex can stimulate strong physical, emotional, and spiritual reactions.

f.   Take care with where you put your attention. Avoid emotionally laden movies, flashing lights, and loud noises.

g.   Do slow belly breathing—as if your lungs were beneath your belly button. This relaxes your diaphragm and helps you stay in touch with your intuition and emotional feelings.

h.   If you need to be cared for, discuss with your ally where you want to go, whom you want to be in attendance, and how to set it up.

If you are in an extreme state, your ally, functioning to the best of his or her ability, may need to get further help for you. In these unlikely circumstances, allow your ally to take you to a hospital crisis center or to contact your primary health care professional to ask for advice.

Many of us feel overwhelmed at some point in life and it is OK to get the help that you need. (As recounted in this book, even though Susan wasn't crazy, she was greatly relieved to have her time in the hospital. It was not a defeat—it was a responsible decision).

If you follow these procedures, you and your support persons will most likely find a way to move through this process with some degree of comfort and without hospitalization. You deserve to feel cared for, as if held in a sanctuary of understanding. You don't have to feel isolated or alienated. You may even feel excited about this process. After all, you are birthing a new and more expanded you!

IF YOU ARE CONCERNED ABOUT
SOMEONE WHO SEEMS TO BE HAVING
A SPIRITUAL EMERGENCY:

1.   Read the above section, "If You Are in Crisis and Believe It Is a Spiritual Emergency."

2.   If you are not this person's appropriate ally, suggest he/she get together with a trusted, supportive friend or relative and begin working together on the above checklist. Reading supportive literature and watching/listening to videos and tapes on the subject are very helpful. (See the list of resources at the end of the Afterword.)

3.   If the person is already under the care of a health care provider and has not yet advised the provider of the crisis, suggest that he/she do so, or offer to do it for him/her. You might give the provider a copy of this book or this section of the book. Not many providers have learned about spiritual emergency, as it was only recently included in professional diagnostic manuals. Be understanding where there is ignorance and help people to become more knowledgeable of the unique needs of the person in crisis.

4.   If the person in crisis is unable to trust anyone, he/she may need immediate professional help. Find a psychiatrist or suitable crisis counselor who is available to assist in a timely manner. You may need to drive the person in crisis directly to the counselor. This is unlikely but can happen. If you sense that the person in crisis could cause self-inflicted harm or hurt others, you need to get him/her to a place where he/she can be cared for responsibly *as soon as possible*.

IF YOU ARE A HEALTH CARE PROVIDER AND ARE
ASSISTING SOMEONE IN SPIRITUAL EMERGENCY:

1.  There are criteria for "spiritual problems" in the
    *DSM-IV* that may assist you in differential diagnosis.
    Spiritual problems, listed as a "z" code, are not them-
    selves indicative of pathology. However, phenomena
    associated with spiritual emergence may be combined
    with other symptoms indicative of pathology.

2.  Rule out physical pathology before making a diagnosis
    of spiritual problems. Some of the symptoms can be a
    result of physiological imbalances, such as uremia, dia-
    betes, toxic states, brain disorders, or cardiac disease.

3.  Consider the following criteria to determine if the per-
    son is experiencing phenomena associated with spiri-
    tual emergence:

    a.  Episodes of unusual experiences that involve
        changes in consciousness and in perceptual, emo-
        tional, cognitive, and psychosomatic functioning,
        and in which there is a significant transpersonal
        emphasis. (See "How to Identify a Spiritual
        Emergency," at the beginning of this Afterword,
        for a list of these criteria.)

    b.  The ability to see the condition as an inner psy-
        chological process and approach it in an inter-
        nalized way; the capacity to form an adequate
        working relationship and maintain the spirit of
        cooperation. These criteria exclude people with
        severe paranoid states, persecutory delusions, and
        hallucinations, and those who consistently use
        the mechanism of projection, exteriorization, and
        acting out (Grof and Grof, 1986).

4.  Be aware that some of the criteria for the diagnosis of psychosis (*DSM-III*, 1980) are observable in episodes where intense spiritual experiences have led to a personal crisis—i.e., a spiritual emergency. For example:

    a.  A disorientation that makes a person less interested in work, social contacts, and self-care.

    b.  A difficulty in communicating about one's experience to others (in spiritual emergency this is the result of the noetic quality of the experience, not symptomatic of confused thinking).

    c.  Dissociation (in spiritual emergency, this is a transitory part of the process of integrating one's experience).

5.  Consider the following four criteria to differentiate brief psychosis from spiritual emergency. If two out of the four are satisfied, a psychotic episode is likely to have a positive outcome, where it contributes to personal development as opposed to a more long-lived erosion of well-being:

    a.  Good pre-episode functioning, as evidenced by no previous history of psychotic episodes, maintenance of a social network of friends, intimate relationships with the opposite sex (or same sex, if homosexual), some success in work or school.

    b.  Acute onset of symptoms during a period of three months or less.

    c.  Stressful precipitants in the psychotic episode such as major life changes: a death in the family, divorce, loss of job, financial problems, beginning a new academic program or job. Major life passages that result in identity crises, such as transition from adolescence to adulthood, should also be considered.

> d. Positive exploratory attitude toward the experience as meaningful, revelatory, growthful. Research has found that a positive attitude toward the psychotic process facilitates integration of the experiences into the person's post-psychotic life (D. Lukoff, 1985).

6. Diagnosis, treatment plan, and prognosis.

   Please be aware that psychiatric medications are not always the optimal choice for individuals in spiritual emergency. Psychiatric drugs tend to inhibit the natural processes through which the self-structure attempts to integrate spiritual experiences. The patient needs to have access to his/her inner process and capacity for self-observation. Some psychiatric medications distort or abort access to these sensitive aspects of the psyche, including the health-giving aspects of emotional catharsis.

   Another significant reason for the minimal use of psychiatric drugs is to allow the person to be observed in his/her more natural state. This is essential for successful diagnosis initially and throughout the process. People in spiritual emergency are rarely a danger to themselves or others unless their process is encumbered by some other pathology.

7. Become familiar with the checklists in this Afterword for the person in spiritual emergency and for those who are concerned about him/her. If you are comfortable with these processes, you may choose to function as one of the person's allies.

It is very difficult to pinpoint the length of time of a spiritual emergency or the outcome. Following the metaphor of birthing, it is safe to say that the more comfortable the person in crisis is, the easier it will be for

205

him/her to open up and go through the transformative process. If the person feels rushed, criticized, inappropriately medicated, or isolated, the process may slow down.

Unlike childbirth, a spiritual emergence process can last minutes, days, or months. Similar to childbirth, something spectacular is being born that will bring more joy into the world!

Statistics show that those who have been through the process have become more compassionate, less materialistic, less fearful of death, more creative, and more motivated to be of service to others.

EMMA BRAGDON, PH.D.

### ADDITIONAL RESOURCES FOR THE PERSON EXPERIENCING OR ASSISTING SPIRITUAL EMERGENCY:

206

1.  *Spiritual Emergency*, by Stanislav Grof, M.D. and Christina Grof, J. P. Tarcher, 1989. Generally available through local libraries and bookstores.

2.  *The Stormy Search for the Self*, by Stanislav Grof, M.D. and Christina Grof, J. P. Tarcher, 1992. Generally available through local libraries and bookstores.

3.  *A Sourcebook for Helping People in Spiritual Emergency*, 1988, and the revised version, *A Sourcebook for Helping People with Spiritual Problems*, 1994, by Emma Bragdon, Ph.D. Available through Upper Access Books, 1-800-356-9315. Dr. Bragdon is available for phone or office consultation. Call 1-800-788-4084, EST.

4.  Spiritual Emergence Network (SEN). This worldwide educational and referral organization was formed in 1980. They have a bookstore, an international team of

support people, and a web site. This is an excellent resource for anyone experiencing or interested in spiritual transition. Phone: 415-648-2610; email: sen@ciis.edu; Internet address: http://elfi.com/sen/.

5.  Thinking Allowed Productions, Berkeley. Videos of a series of thought-provoking interviews with pioneering health professionals in the field of transpersonal psychology. Especially recommended is "Spiritual Psychology," with Frances Vaughan, Ph.D., and "Visionary Experience or Psychosis," with John Weir Perry, M.D. Call 1-800-999-4415.

6.  New Dimensions, San Francisco. Audiotaped interviews with authors, teachers, and health professionals addressing many meaningful and contemporary issues, including spiritual crisis. Call 415-563-8899.

7.  Mystic Fire Video. Carries a broad selection of videos on topics related to transformative visions, alternate realities, and creativity. Call 1-800-292-9001.

8.  Physicians and other health care providers interested in further research should consult books by John Weir Perry, M.D. and Stanislav Grof, M.D.

208

# BEYOND WORDS PUBLISHING, INC.

MISSION STATEMENT

*Inspire to Integrity*

OUR DECLARED VALUES

*We give to all of life as life has given us.*
*We honor all relationships.*
*Trust and stewardship are integral to fulfilling dreams.*
*Collaboration is essential to create miracles.*
*Creativity and aesthetics nourish the soul.*
*Unlimited thinking is fundamental.*
*Living your passion is vital.*
*Joy and humor open our hearts to growth.*
*It is important to remind ourselves of love.*